A BOOK OF LOVE

AN ANTHOLOGY

OF WORDS AND PICTURES

COMPILED BY

JOHN HADFIELD

1958

LONDON : EDWARD HULTON

FIRST PUBLISHED IN 1958 BY

E. HULTON & COMPANY LIMITED

HULTON HOUSE · FLEET STREET

LONDON E.C.4

PRINTED IN GREAT BRITAIN AT

THE CURWEN PRESS · PLAISTOW E.13

Sylvia

To whom this book was surely dedicated,

Brian. Jan 2nd, 1959.

————————

(To be read during prolonged poker sessions.)

A BOOK OF LOVE

An Anthology of Words and Pictures

THE PAINTER AND HIS WIFE: PAINTING BY SIR PETER PAUL RUBENS, *c.* 1609

Now what is love, I pray thee tell?
It is that fountain and that well
Where pleasure and repentance dwell.
It is perhaps that sauncing bell
That tolls all into heaven or hell:
And this is love, as I hear tell.

Yet what is love, I pray thee say?
It is a work on holy day.
It is December matched with May,
When lusty bloods in fresh array
Hear ten months after of the play:
And this is love, as I hear say.

Yet what is love, I pray thee sain?
It is a sunshine mixed with rain.
It is a tooth-ache, or like pain;
It is a game where none doth gain;
The lass saith No, and would full fain:
And this is love, as I hear sain.

Yet what is love, I pray thee say?
It is a yea, it is a nay,
A pretty kind of sporting fray;
It is a thing will soon away;
Then take the vantage while you may:
And this is love, as I hear say.

Yet what is love, I pray thee show?
A thing that creeps, it cannot go;
A prize that passeth to and fro;
A thing for one, a thing for mo;
And he that proves must find it so:
And this is love, sweet friend, I trow.

SIR WALTER RALEIGH
in *The Phoenix Nest,* 1593

INTRODUCTION

LOVE is a much abused word. 'If used with any seriousness,' wrote
Walter de la Mare in the introduction to his own encyclopaedic
anthology of the subject, 'response to it in company is unlikely to
be encouraging. It will share the mental recoil and uneasiness that
may follow the mention of God, or sin, or soul, or death . . . We
become self-conscious, though of which self we may fail to enquire.'

Self-consciousness may be an embarrassment. It may also be, as
Walter de la Mare hints, something quite different – an awareness
of the real nature of one's self. In choosing and developing the theme
for the fourth of my 'anthologies of words and pictures' I decided
to risk the superficial unease which the word *love* induces, provided
I could in some degree increase my own awareness – and perhaps
some other people's – of its real meaning.

Awareness – like love itself – is not something that can be taught:
nor is it something which can be explained. My approach to the
subject therefore is experimental rather than didactic, intuitive rather
than definitive. Sir Walter Raleigh, in the poem which prefaces the
book, comes as near to defining love as I would wish to do. My aim
is the less ambitious one of *illustrating* – illustrating the need of love,
the search for love, and some of the forms of love, through a free
association of pictures, poems and passages of prose.

The choice of illustrations – text and picture – is governed entirely
by my own aesthetic and emotional responses. Not for a moment
would I suggest that this book contains the most perfect love lyrics
or that the pictures are all masterpieces. Love is, to borrow the
phrase of the patent-medicine vendor, an almost universal complaint;
and its symptoms can sometimes be as faithfully diagnosed in a
Victorian ballad as in a metaphysical poem by Donne. Most of the
great paintings and sculptures which are explicitly concerned with

love – Cupid and Psyche, Venus and Adonis, and the like – have a purely academic interest to most of us: they fail to touch the emotions. There are, however, at all levels of achievement, works of art which have been inspired and executed with love – with passion, emotional fire, or genuine sentiment. One's awareness of this, and one's response, is, of course, personal and unpredictable.

Few people would deny that the painting by Rubens which is reproduced here as the frontispiece is a passionate celebration of the physical and emotional reality of marriage. But I do not necessarily expect others to share my own response to the sexual vitality in the rock-painting from the Sahara, the tender sentiment of Mrs. Carpenter's water-colour, 'The Love Letter', or the spirituality and other-worldliness of the portrait by Dirk Bouts. Whether or not you – the reader, the other pair of eyes – respond to or reject these images and implications, is a matter of taste, temperament and experience.

I have assembled my *collages* of words and pictures within the simple and conventional framework of the Four Seasons, partly because I wanted to avoid the definitions implied by such headings as Mother Love, Spiritual Love, and so on, and partly because the different poetic 'climates' of love can obviously be related to the seasons of the year.

This arrangement has also enabled me to weave together the varied strands of experience spun by spirit and sex, body and soul, or, as our forebears used to call them, the Sacred and the Profane. Spring is traditionally 'the pretty ringtime'; but the springtime of life is also that state of innocence when 'eternity was manifest in the light of the day, and something infinite behind everything appeared'. Autumn is not merely the season of fruition, or, conversely, of the falling leaf: it can also be a time of accomplishment, when love flowers in industry and creation; or it can be a time when, as

Santayana says, 'Nature is a second mistress that consoles us for the loss of a first'. And in winter those who have the blessed fortune to sit in companionship by the fireside need feel no lack of devotion to their Darby or their Joan if they become increasingly aware, in Kathleen Raine's words, that

> Like the sea-sounding blood that children hear
> At night when the ear's shell is held to sleep,
> Infinity flows round us with the dark
> And heaven hangs behind the window-curtain.

I have said that I will attempt no definition of love, but as I turn the completed pages of this scrapbook – it is no more than that – I *do* see in its sequence of thoughts and images a reflection of Coleridge's dictum: 'Love is a desire of the whole being to be united to some thing, or some being, felt necessary to its completeness, by the most perfect means that nature permits.' Over two thousand years earlier Plato had expressed the same sense in the statement that 'the desire and pursuit of the whole is called love?'

An eminent rationalist of our own time, Bertrand Russell, has written: 'Love is something far more than desire for sexual intercourse; it is the principal means of escape from the loneliness which afflicts most men and women throughout the greater part of their lives. There is a deep-seated fear, in most people, of the cold world and the possible cruelty of the herd; there is a longing for affection, which is often concealed by roughness, boorishness or a bullying manner in men, and by nagging and scolding in women. Passionate mutual love while it lasts puts an end to this feeling; it breaks down the hard walls of the ego, producing a new being composed of two in one. Nature did not construct human beings to stand alone, since they cannot fulfil her biological purpose except with the help of another; and civilized people cannot fully satisfy their sexual instinct without love. The instinct is not completely satisfied unless a man's whole being, mental quite as much as physical, enters into the relation. Those who have never known the deep intimacy and the intense companionship of happy mutual love have missed the best thing that life has to give.'

As far as it goes, that is in accord with Coleridge's and Plato's definitions. But it does not go as far as infinity! And 'infinite love', to quote Traherne, 'cannot be expressed in finite room, but must have infinite places wherein to utter and shew itself'. Union with nature, with the spirit of a place, or with God, can be as compelling a call as sexual desire.

Readers of this book who happen to be – let them cherish the moment! – sun-bathing in the midsummer of love, when 'the heart has, as it were, filled up the moulds of the imagination,' may be a little disconcerted to find in these pages an undercurrent of yearning, of questioning, of seeking for 'something I can never find . . . in the bottom of my mind'. Is it mere pessimism which prompts this search, these doubts, this awareness of incompletion?

> Yes! in the sea of life enisled,
> With echoing straits between us thrown,
> Dotting the shoreless watery wild,
> We mortal millions live *alone*.
> The islands feel the enclasping flow,
> And then their endless bounds they know.
>
> But when the moon their hollows lights,
> And they are swept by balms of spring,
> And in their glens, on starry nights,
> The nightingales divinely sing;
> And lovely notes, from shore to shore,
> Across the sounds and channels pour –

Oh! then a longing like despair
Is to their farthest caverns sent;
For surely once, they feel, we were
Parts of a single continent . . .

Matthew Arnold, perhaps, *was* a pessimist. But one does not have to be a pessimist to accept his view of the separation of island from island, of man from man, and of man from woman. One does not have to be a pessimist to go further, and recognize the separation of the visible world from what we call God. Traherne was no pessimist: he roundly declared: 'Infinite wants satisfied produce infinite joys . . . You must want like a god that you may be satisfied like God.'

In a few little mirrors set at different levels and various angles I have tried to reflect a few of the aspects of love – of the desire of the whole being to be united to some thing, or some being, whether it be God or the girl next door. If I have sometimes tried to catch a glimpse of infinity, I have not ignored the ritual of the dance, the sentimental exchanges of the Valentine and the love letter, the symbolism of fruit and flower, and the common currency of popular song. If the reader is sometimes made aware of the melancholy that echoes from island to island across 'the unplumb'd, salt, estranging sea,' I hope he or she will also gain some reassurance of Hazlitt's statement that 'perfect love reposes on the object of its choice like the halcyon on the wave, and the air of heaven is around it'.

J.H.

ACKNOWLEDGEMENTS

THE COMPILER AND PUBLISHERS make acknowledgement of the generous facilities afforded by the galleries, museums, artists, photographers and collectors named in the Notes on the Illustrations. Almost all the works reproduced in colour were specially photographed for this book, and the compiler wishes to express his thanks to the photographers, especially Miss Eileen Tweedy and Fine Art Engravers. He also acknowledges with thanks the help given to him by Miss Jean Pullen and Mr. W. D. Marshall.

For permission to quote copyright passages acknowledgement is made to Mr. Conrad Aiken for the poem 'Annihilation'; to Messrs. Basil Blackwell & Mott for a poem by E. H. W. Meyerstein; to Messrs. Jonathan Cape for a poem by Emily Dickinson, for 'The Album' by Mr. C. Day Lewis and for a passage from Kilvert's *Diary*; to the Bodley Head for two passages from *Love and Death* by Llewelyn Powys; to Messrs. Chappell & Company for the refrain from Mr. Noël Coward's 'Dance, Little Lady'; to the Clarendon Press for the passage from Robert Bridges's translation of Plato's *Symposium*; to the Cresset Press for two poems by Mrs. Frances Cornford and a poem by Miss Ruth Pitter; to Messrs. Francis, Day & Hunter for the words of 'Why am I always a Bridesmaid'; to the Trustees of the estate of Walter de la Mare and Messrs. Faber & Faber for a poem by Walter de la Mare; to Messrs. J. M. Dent & Sons for two poems by Dylan Thomas and a passage from *Immanence* by Evelyn Underhill; to Messrs. Faber & Faber for a poem by Mr. W. H. Auden; to the Executors of the estate of Mrs. John Freeman for two poems by John Freeman; to Mr. Robert Frost and Messrs. Jonathan Cape for two poems by Mr. Frost; to Miss Viola Garvin for an extract from 'Holy Thorn'; to Dr. Philip Gosse for a poem by Sir Edmund Gosse; to Mr. Robert Graves and Messrs.

Cassell & Company for two poems by Mr. Graves; to Messrs. Hamish Hamilton for a poem by Miss Kathleen Raine; to the Trustees of the Hardy Estate and Messrs. Macmillan & Company for two poems by Thomas Hardy; to Messrs. Rupert Hart-Davies for a poem by Mr. Laurence Whistler; to Messrs. Heinemann for a passage from Gilbert Cannan's translation of *Jean Christophe* by Romain Rolland; to Messrs. Hodder & Stoughton for a passage from Miss Helen Keller's *Autobiography*; to the Hogarth Press for the poem 'Do not expect again a phoenix hour' by Mr. C. Day Lewis; to the estate of Mrs. Frieda Lawrence for four poems by D. H. Lawrence; to Mr. Laurie Lee for a poem from *The Bloom of Candles*; to Miss Anna McMullen for the poem 'By the River'; to Messrs. John Murray for two poems by Mr. John Betjeman; to Messrs. Pearn, Pollinger & Higham and Messrs. Methuen for a poem by Miss Dorothy Parker; to the Peterborough Museum Society for the poem, 'My love is as sweet as a beanfield in blossom' by John Clare; to Messrs. Routledge & Kegan Paul for a letter by John Clare; to Messrs. Sidgwick & Jackson for a poem by John Drinkwater; to the Society of Authors and Mrs. Cicely Binyon for poems by Laurence Binyon; to Mrs. Yeats and Messrs. Macmillan & Company for a poem from W. B. Yeats's *Collected Poems* and a passage from his *Ideas of Good and Evil*.

NOTE. *The reference at the end of each passage is, in almost every instance, to the date and place of its first appearance in book form. Where lines have been omitted this is indicated by dots, thus . . . The spelling and punctuation of the text has been modernized throughout, except in the Dyer inscription quoted on page 235. In order to allow as much room as possible for the illustrations, notes on their sources are printed at the end of the book.*

CONTENTS

O LOVE, who in my breast's most noble part
　　Did'st that fair image lodge, that form divine,
　　In whom the sum of heavenly graces shine,
And there engrav'dst it with thy golden dart:

Now, mighty workman, help me by thy art
　　(Since my dull pen trembles to strike a line)
　　That I on paper copy the design
By thee expressed so lively in my heart.

Lend me, when I this great attempt do try,
　　A feather from thy wings, that, whilst to write
My hand's employed, my thoughts may soar on high;
　　Thy torch, which fires our hearts and burns so bright,
My darker fancy let its flame supply,
　　And through my numbers dart celestial light.

PHILIP AYRES, *Lyric Poems*, 1687

SPRING

NOTHING is so beautiful as spring—
   When weeds, in wheels, shoot long and lovely and lush;
   Thrush's eggs look little low heavens, and thrush
Through the echoing timber does so rinse and wring
The ear, it strikes like lightnings to hear him sing;
   The glassy peartree leaves and blooms, they brush
   The descending blue; that blue is all in a rush
With richness; the racing lambs too have fair their fling.

What is all this juice and all this joy?
   A strain of the earth's sweet being in the beginning
In Eden garden.—Have, get, before it cloy,
   Before it cloud, Christ, lord, and sour with sinning,
Innocent mind and Mayday in girl and boy,
   Most, O maid's child, thy choice and worthy the winning.

GERARD MANLEY HOPKINS
in *Poets and Poetry of the Century*, 1894
(written 1877)

THE NEW-BORN BABY'S SONG

WHEN I was twenty inches long,
I could not hear the thrushes' song;
The radiance of morning skies
Was most displeasing to my eyes.

For loving looks, caressing words,
I cared no more than sun or birds;
But I could bite my mother's breast,
And that made up for all the rest.

FRANCES CORNFORD
Autumn Midnight, 1923

MOTHER AND CHILD: GOUACHE BY PABLO PICASSO, 1905

YOUNG HARE: WATER-COLOUR BY ALBRECHT DÜRER, 1502

I COME IN THE LITTLE THINGS

I COME in the little things,
Saith the Lord:
Not borne on morning wings
Of majesty, but I have set My Feet
Amidst the delicate and bladed wheat
That springs triumphant in the furrowed sod.
There do I dwell, in weakness and in power;
Not broken or divided, saith our God!
In your strait garden plot I come to flower:
About your porch My Vine
Meek, fruitful, doth entwine;
Waits, at the threshold, Love's appointed hour.

I come in the little things,
Saith the Lord:
Yea! on the glancing wings
Of eager birds, the softly pattering feet
Of furred and gentle beasts, I come to meet
Your hard and wayward heart. In brown bright eyes
That peep from out the brake, I stand confest.
On every nest
Where feathery Patience is content to brood
And leaves her pleasure for the high emprise
Of motherhood—
There doth My Godhead rest . . .

EVELYN UNDERHILL
Immanence, 1913

POINT OF ORIGIN

Do you remember, when you were a child,
Nothing in the world seemed strange to you?
You perceived, for the first time, shapes already familiar,
And seeing, you knew that you had always known
The lichen on the rock, fern-leaves, the flowers of thyme,
As if the elements newly met in your body,
Caught up into the momentary vortex of your living
Still kept the knowledge of a former state,
In you retained recollection of cloud and ocean
The branching tree, the dancing flame.

Now when nature's darkness seems strange to you,
And you walk, an alien, in the streets of cities,
Remember earth breathed you into her with the air,
   with the sun's rays,
Laid you in her waters asleep, to dream
With the brown trout among the milfoil roots,
From substance of star and ocean fashioned you,
At the same source conceived you
As sun and foliage, fish and stream . . .

KATHLEEN RAINE
'Message from Home'
The Year One, 1952

JERUSALEM IN KENTISH-TOWN

THE fields from Islington to Marybone,
    To Primrose Hill and Saint John's Wood,
Were builded over with pillars of gold;
    And there Jerusalem's pillars stood.

Her Little-ones ran on the fields,
    The Lamb of God among them seen,
And fair Jerusalem, his Bride,
    Among the little meadows green.

Pancrass and Kentish-town repose
    Among her golden pillars high,
Among her golden arches which
    Shine upon the starry sky.

The Jew's-harp-house and the Green Man,
    The Ponds where Boys to bathe delight,
The fields of Cows by Willan's farm,
    Shine in Jerusalem's pleasant sight.

She walks upon our meadows green;
    The Lamb of God walks by her side,
And every English Child is seen
    Children of Jesus and his Bride . . .

WILLIAM BLAKE, *Jerusalem*, 1804–20

ESTATE OF INNOCENCE

I WAS a little stranger, which, at my entrance into the world, was saluted and surrounded with innumerable joys. My knowledge was divine . . . My very ignorance was advantageous. I seemed as one brought into the Estate of Innocence. All things were spotless and pure and glorious: yea, and infinitely mine, and joyful and precious. I knew not that there were any sins, or complaints or laws. I dreamed not of poverties, contentions or vices. All tears and quarrels were hidden from mine eyes. Everything was at rest, free and immortal. I knew nothing of sickness or death or rents or exaction, either for tribute or bread. In the absence of these I was entertained like an angel with the works of God in their splendour and glory, I saw all in the peace of Eden; heaven and earth did sing my Creator's praises, and could not make more melody to Adam than to me. All time was eternity, and a perpetual Sabbath. Is it not strange that an infant should be heir of the whole world, and see those mysteries which the books of the learned never unfold?

THOMAS TRAHERNE, *Centuries of Meditations*, 1908
(written *c.* 1670)

Ann Moore

Here in her Ashes A young phenix lyes
But An Æternall phenix thence Shall Rise
propriety in Blisse Age pleads in Vain
To Little ones Gods kingdom doth pertain
See here the Best ith least of Adams Race
Whole heauen Contracted in a Babe of Grace
But Such perfections least We adore
We only See to imitate and See no more
View here Mysterious fates to knowing Rage
An infant body had A soule at Age
And yet A Body so refind and Tryed
in sicknefs deaths Alembicke Rarefyed
That th'inmate soule grown Jealous of its Host
Returnd to God where left Dust to Dust
   Read then deaths Impartiall Rod
   This liud thus Dyed a Lambe of God

   The Cask decayes The Jewell fled
   The soule at Rest The Rest is dead

Obijt Decimo Julij
1683

MONUMENT TO A CHILD IN PLUMPTON CHURCH, NORTHAMPTONSHIRE, 1683

CHILD WITH BIRD AND APPLE: PAINTING BY CAESAR VAN EVERDINGEN, 1664

PHILIP SPARROW

. . . It had a velvet cap,
And would sit upon my lap,
And seek after small worms,
And sometime white bread crumbs;
And many times and oft
Between my breastës soft
It would lie and rest;
It was proper and prest.
Sometimes he would gasp
When he saw a wasp;
A fly or a gnat,
He would fly at that;
And prettily he would pant
When he saw an ant;
Lord, how he would pry
After a butterfly!
Lord, how he would hop
After the grasshop!
And when I said, 'Phip Phip!'
Then he would leap and skip,
And take me by the lip.
Alas, it will be slo,
That Philip is gone me fro . . .

JOHN SKELTON
The Book of Philip Sparrow, 1550

GOLDEN DAYS

See with what simplicity
This nymph begins her golden days!
In the green grass she loves to lie,
And there with her fair aspect tames
The wilder flowers, and gives them names:
But only with the roses plays;
      And them does tell
What colour best becomes them, and what smell.

Who can foretell for what high cause
This darling of the Gods was born?
Yet this is she whose chaster laws
The wanton Love shall one day fear,
And, under her command severe,
See his bow broke, and ensigns torn.
      Happy, who can
Appease this virtuous enemy of man!

O then let me in time compound
And parley with those conquering eyes,
Ere they have tried their force to wound;
Ere with their glancing wheels they drive
In triumph over hearts that strive,
And them that yield but more despise:
      Let me be laid
Where I may see thy glories from some shade.

Meantime, whilst every verdant thing
Itself does at thy beauty charm,
Reform the errors of the spring;
Make that the tulips may have share
Of sweetness, seeing they are fair;
And roses of their thorns disarm;
       But most, procure
That violets may a longer age endure.

But O, young beauty of the woods,
Whom Nature courts with fruits and flowers,
Gather the flowers, but spare the buds,
Lest Flora, angry at thy crime
To kill her infants in their prime,
Do quickly make the example yours;
       And ere we see
Nip in the blossom all our hopes and thee.

ANDREW MARVELL
'The Picture of little T.C.
in a Prospect of Flowers'
Miscellaneous Poems, 1681

RADIANCE OF EDEN

BRIGHT through the valley gallops the brooklet;
   Over the welkin travels the cloud;
Touched by the zephyr, dances the harebell;
   Cuckoo sits somewhere, singing so loud;
Swift o'er the meadows glitter the starlings,
   Striking their wings, all the flock at a stroke;
Under the chestnuts new bees are swarming,
   Rising and falling like magical smoke.
Two little children, seeing and hearing,
   Hand in hand wander, shout, laugh, and sing:
Lo, in their bosoms, wild with the marvel,
   Love, like the crocus, is come ere the Spring.
Young men and women, noble and tender,
   Yearn for each other, faith truly plight,
Promise to cherish, comfort and honour;
   Vow that makes duty one with delight.
Oh, but the glory, found in no story,
   Radiance of Eden unquenched by the Fall;
Few may remember, none may reveal it,
   This the first first-love, the first love of all!

COVENTRY PATMORE
Tamerton Church-Tower, and other Poems, 1853

THE LITTLE DANCERS

LONELY, save for a few faint stars, the sky
Dreams; and lonely, below, the little street
Into its gloom retires, secluded and shy.
Scarcely the dumb roar enters this soft retreat;
And all is dark, save where come flooding rays
From a tavern-window: there, to the brisk measure
Of an organ that down in an alley merrily plays,
Two children, all alone and no one by,
Holding their tattered frocks, through an airy maze
Of motion lightly threaded with nimble feet
Dance sedately: face to face they gaze,
Their eyes shining, grave with a perfect pleasure.

LAURENCE BINYON
London Visions, 1898

31

THE YOUTH WHO CARRIED A LIGHT

I saw him pass as the new day dawned,
   Murmuring some musical phrase;
Horses were drinking and floundering in the pond,
   And the tired stars thinned their gaze;
Yet these were not the spectacles at all that he conned,
   But an inner one, giving out rays.

Such was the thing in his eye, walking there,
   The very and visible thing,
A close light, displacing the gray of the morning air,
   And the tokens that the dark was taking wing;
And was it not the radiance of a purpose rare
   That might ripe to its accomplishing?

What became of that light? I wonder still its fate!
   Was it quenched at its very apogee?
Did it struggle frail and frailer to a beam emaciate?
   Did it thrive till matured in verity?
Or did it travel on, to be a new young dreamer's freight,
   And thence on infinitely?

THOMAS HARDY
Moments of Vision, 1917

DESIRE

FOR giving me desire,
An eager thirst, a burning ardent fire,
A virgin infant flame,
A love with which into the world I came,
An inward hidden heavenly love,
Which in my soul did work and move,
And ever, ever, me inflame
With restless longing, heavenly avarice,
That never could be satisfied,
That did incessantly a Paradise
Unknown suggest, and something undescried
Discern, and bear me to it; be
Thy name for ever praised by me . . .

This soaring, sacred thirst,
Ambassador of bliss, approachëd first,
Making a place in me
That made me apt to prize, and taste, and see;
For not the objects but the sense
Of things doth bliss to souls dispense,
And make it, Lord, like thee.
Sense, feeling, taste, complacency, and sight,
These are the true and real joys,
The living, flowing, inward, melting, bright,
And heavenly pleasures; all the rest are toys;
All which are founded in desire,
As light in flame, and heat in fire.

THOMAS TRAHERNE, *Poems of Felicity*, 1903
(written *c.* 1670)

33

A WEAPON FOR THE WOMAN

When creatures first were formed,
　　They had, by Nature's laws,
The bulls, their horns; the horses, hoofs;
　　The lions, teeth and paws:
To hares she swiftness gave;
　　To fishes fins assigned;
To birds, their wings: so no defence
　　Was left for womankind.
But, to supply that want,
　　She gave her such a face
Which makes the bold, the fierce, the swift,
　　To stoop and plead for grace.

GEFFREY WHITNEY
Emblems, and Other Devices, 1586

LA TOILETTE DU MATIN: PAINTING BY JEAN-BAPTISTE-SIMÉON CHARDIN, 1741

ANN AND JANE TAYLOR: PAINTING BY ISAAC TAYLOR, THEIR FATHER, 1791

DOUBLE CHERRY

We, Hermia, like two artificial gods,
Have with our neelds created both one flower,
Both on one sampler, sitting on one cushion,
Both warbling of one song, both in one key;
As if our hands, our sides, voices, and minds,
Had been incorporate. So we grew together,
Like to a double cherry, seeming parted;
But yet a union in partition,
Two lovely berries moulded on one stem:
So, with two seeming bodies, but one heart;
Two of the first, like coats in heraldry,
Due but to one, and crownëd with one crest.

WILLIAM SHAKESPEARE
A Midsummer Night's Dream, 1600

SWEET, CARELESS YOUTH

YOUTH, O sweet, careless Youth, flooding the vein
With easy blood, what time the body knows
Scarce that it is, so brimmingly life glows
Within it, and its motions are like words
Born happy on the lips, and like the birds
On April-blossomed boughs rich fancies throng
The mind's exuberance and spill in song,
I think my heart back into all the bloom
And feel it fresh. As one that enters home,
I am there: the shyness, and the secret flame
Of ecstasy that knew not any name,
The wild heart-eating fevers, the young tears,
The absorbed soul, the trouble, and the fears
Wide as the night, the joy without a thought
Meeting the morning, – Time has never taught
My heart to lose them. Still I smell that rose
Of so inscrutable sweetness; and still glows
The glory of the wonder when I first
Heard the enchanted poets, and they burst
In song upon my spirit, as if before
No one had ever passed that magic door,
But for me, first in all the world, they sang . . .
Sweetest of all things, Youth, sweet in the pang
As in the pleasure, you are in me yet,
Changed as the grape to wine: could I forget,
Then were this hand dust. In those yesterdays
Memory happy and familiar strays,
Exploring hours that, long in shadow lain,
Come effortlessly all distinct again,

As in my light boat I would track the banks
Of narrow streams that rippled past the ranks
Of yellow-flowered reeds, and knew not where
They led me, for no human sound was there,
But the shy wings were near me, and I to them,
And the wild earth was round me as in a dream
And I was melted into it. I can hear,
Lost in the green, bright silence, where I steer
Beneath gold shadows wavering on my arm
The water saying over its low charm
Among the reeds, and, dreading to disturb
The mirror of the blossomed willow-herb,
Drink it into my heart. O idle hours,
Floating with motion like the summer towers
Of cloud in the blue noon, I have not drained
Your fullness yet, for all that care has rained
Upon defeated days of dark sundown,
Like burial of all beauty and all renown,
When the spirit sits within its fortalice
And watches mute . . .

LAURENCE BINYON
from 'Westward'
The Secret, 1920

A FRIEND

. . . IF ever I tasted a disembodied transport on earth, it was in those friendships which I entertained at school, before I dreamt of any maturer feeling . . . I loved my friend for his gentleness, his candour, his truth, his good repute, his freedom even from my own livelier manner, his calm and reasonable kindness. It was not any particular talent that attracted me to him, or anything striking whatsoever. I should say, in one word, it was his goodness. I doubt whether he ever had a conception of a tithe of the regard and respect I entertained for him; and I smile to think of the perplexity (though he never showed it) which he probably felt sometimes at my enthusiastic expressions; for I thought him a kind of angel . . . With the other boys I played antics, and rioted in fantastic jests; but in his society, or whenever I thought of him, I fell into a kind of Sabbath state of bliss; and I am sure I could have died for him.

I experienced this delightful affection towards three successive schoolfellows . . .

LEIGH HUNT, *Autobiography*, 1850

WHAT tenderness and what devotion; what illimitable confidence; infinite revelations of inmost thoughts; what ecstatic present and romantic future; what bitter estrangements and what melting reconciliations; what scenes of wild recrimination, agitating explanations, passionate correspondence; what insane sensitiveness, and what frantic sensibility; what earthquakes of the heart and whirlwinds of the soul are confined in that simple phrase, a schoolboy's friendship!

BENJAMIN DISRAELI, *Coningsby*, 1844

HEAD OF A BOY: DRAWING IN CHALK BY FRANÇOIS BOUCHER, EIGHTEENTH CENTURY

JEUNES BAIGNEURS BRETONS: PAINTING BY PAUL GAUGUIN, 1888

THE UNKNOWN JOY

WHEN we were idlers with the loitering rills,
The need of human love we little noted:
Our love was nature; and the peace that floated
On the white mist, and dwelt upon the hills,
To sweet accord subdued our wayward wills:
One soul was ours, one mind, one heart devoted,
That, wisely doating, asked not why it doated,
And ours the unknown joy, which knowing kills.
But now I find how dear thou wert to me;
That man is more than half of nature's treasure,
Of that fair beauty which no eye can see,
Of that sweet music which no ear can measure;
And now the streams may sing for others' pleasure,
The hills sleep on in their eternity.

HARTLEY COLERIDGE
'To a Friend', *Poems*, 1833

FIRST FRUIT

SHE would spend the day prowling round the garden, eating, watching, laughing, picking at the grapes on the vines like a thrush, secretly plucking a peach from the trellis, climbing a plum-tree, or giving it a little surreptitious shake as she passed to bring down a rain of the golden mirabelles which melt in the mouth like scented honey. Or she would pick the flowers, although that was forbidden: quickly she would pluck a rose that she had been coveting all day, and run away with it to the arbour at the end of the garden. Then she would bury her little nose in the delicious-scented flower, and kiss it, and bite it, and suck it: and then she would conceal her booty, and hide it in her bosom between her little breasts, at the wonder of whose coming she would gaze in eager fondness.

ROMAIN ROLLAND, *Jean Christophe*, 1904
translated by Gilbert Cannan

GOLDEN PAVILIONS

To the heart of youth the world is a highwayside.
   Passing for ever, he fares; and on either hand,
Deep in the gardens, golden pavilions hide,
   Nestle in orchard bloom, and far on the level land
Call him with lighted lamp in the eventide.

Thick as the stars at night when the moon is down,
   Pleasures assail him. He to his nobler fate
Fares; and but waves a hand as he passes on,
   Cries but a wayside word to her at the garden gate,
Sings but a boyish stave, and his face is gone.

ROBERT LOUIS STEVENSON
Songs of Travel, 1896

FLAPPER

LOVE has crept out of her sealëd heart
   As a field-bee, black and amber,
   Breaks from the winter-cell, to clamber
Up the warm grass where the sunbeams start.

Mischief has come in her dawning eyes,
   And a glint of coloured iris brings
   Such as lies along the folded wings
Of the bee before he flies.

Who, with a ruffling, careful breath,
   Has opened the wings of the wild young sprite?
   Has fluttered her spirit to stumbling flight
In her eyes, as a young bee stumbleth?

Love makes the burden of her voice.
   The hum of his heavy, staggering wings
   Sets quivering with wisdom the common things
That she says, and her words rejoice.

D. H. LAWRENCE, *New Poems*, 1918

LE CHAPEAU AUX ROSES: PAINTING BY SUZANNE EISENDIECK, *c.* 1930

MAURICE, COUNT OF NASSAU, AGED 14: PAINTING BY UNKNOWN DUTCH ARTIST, 1580

KNIGHT-ERRANT

AND now, his armour being scoured, his head-piece improved to a helmet, his horse and himself new-named, he perceived he wanted nothing but a lady, on whom he might bestow the empire of his heart; for he was sensible that a knight-errant without a mistress was a tree without either fruit or leaves, and a body without a soul. 'Should I,' said he to himself, 'by good or ill fortune chance to encounter some giant, as it is common in knight errantry, and happen to lay him prostrate on the ground, transfixed with my lance, or cleft in two, or in short, overcome and have him at my mercy, would it not be proper to have some lady to whom I may send him as a trophy of my valour? That, when he comes into her presence, throwing himself at her feet, he may thus make his humble submission: "Lady, I am the giant Caraculiambro, lord of the island of Malindrania, vanquished in single combat by that never-deservedly-enough-extolled knight-errant Don Quixote de la Mancha, who has commanded me to cast myself most humbly at your feet, that it may please your honour to dispose of me according to your will."' Oh! how elevated was the Knight with the conceit of this imaginary submission of the giant; especially having bethought himself of a person on whom he might confer the title of mistress! which, it is believed, happened thus. Near the place where he lived dwelt a good likely country lass, for whom he had formerly had a sort of an inclination, though it is believed she never heard of it, nor regarded it in the least. Her name was Aldonza Lorenzo, and this was she whom he thought he might entitle to the sovereignty of his heart . . .

MIGUEL DE CERVANTES SAAVEDRA
The History of Don Quixote, 1605–15
translated by Peter Motteux

49

A BEGINNING

THAT was her beginning, an apparition
of rose in the unbreathed airs of his love,
her heart revealed by the wash of summer
sprung from her childhood's shallow stream.

Then it was that she put up her hair,
inscribed her eyes with a look of grief,
while her limbs grew as curious as coral branches,
her breast full of secrets.

But the boy, confused in his day's desire,
was searching for herons, his fingers bathed
in the green of walnuts, or watching at night
the Great Bear spin from the maypole star.

It was then that he paused in the death of a game,
felt the hook of her hair on his swimming throat,
saw her mouth at large in the dark river
flushed like a salmon.

But he covered his face and hid his joy
in a wild-goose web of false directions,
and hunted the woods for eggs and glow-worms,
for rabbits tasteless as moss.

And she walked in fields where the crocuses
branded her feet, where mares' tails sprang
from the prancing lake, and the salty grasses
surged round her stranded body.

LAURIE LEE, *The Bloom of Candles*, 1947

FIRST FLAME

Ah, I remember well – and how can I
But ever more remember well – when first
Our flame began, when scarce we knew what was
The flame we felt; when as we sat and sighed,
And looked upon each other, and conceived
Not what we ailed, yet something we did ail,
And yet were well, and yet we were not well,
And what was our disease we could not tell.
Then would we kiss, then sigh, then look: and thus
In that first garden of our simpleness
We spent our childhood: but when years began
To reap the fruit of knowledge, ah, how then
Would she with graver looks, with sweet stern brow,
Check my presumption and my forwardness;
Yet still would give me flowers, still would shew
What she would have me, yet not have me, know.

SAMUEL DANIEL
Hymen's Triumph, 1623

INDOOR GAMES

IN among the silver birches winding ways of tarmac wander
And the signs to Bussock Bottom, Tussock Wood and Windy Brake,
Gabled lodges, tile-hung churches, catch the lights of our Lagonda
As we drive to Wendy's party, lemon curd and Christmas cake.
Rich the makes of motor whirring, past the pine-plantation purring
                Come up, Hupmobile, Delage!
Short the way your chauffeurs travel, crunching over private gravel
                Each from out his warm garáge.

Oh but Wendy, when the carpet yielded to my indoor pumps
There you stood, your gold hair streaming, handsome in the hall-light
    gleaming
There you looked and there you led me off into the game of clumps
Then the new Victrola playing and your funny uncle saying
'Choose your partners for a fox-trot! Dance until its *tea* o'clock!
'Come on, young 'uns, foot it featly!' Was it chance that paired us neatly,
                I, who loved you so completely,
You, who pressed me closely to you, hard against your party frock?

'Meet me when you've finished eating!' So we met and no one found us.
Oh that dark and furry cupboard while the rest played hide and seek!
Holding hands our two hearts beating in the bedroom silence round us,
Holding hands and hardly hearing sudden footsteps, thud and shriek.
Love that lay too deep for kissing – 'Where IS Wendy? Wendy's
    missing!'
                Love so pure it *had* to end,
Love so strong that I was frighten'd when you gripped my fingers tight
    and
                Hugging, whispered 'I'm your friend.'

Good-bye Wendy! Send the fairies, pinewood elf and larch tree gnome,
Spingle-spangled stars are peeping at the lush Lagonda creeping
Down the winding ways of tarmac to the leaded lights of home.
There, among the silver birches, all the bells of all the churches
Sounded in the bath-waste running out into the frosty air.
Wendy speeded my undressing, Wendy is the sheet's caressing
              Wendy bending gives a blessing,
Holds me as I drift to dreamland, safe inside my slumberwear.

JOHN BETJEMAN
'Indoor Games near Newbury'
Selected Poems, 1948

ECSTASY

THE daffodils were nodding in bright yellow clumps in the little garden plots before the almshouse doors. And there a great ecstasy of happiness fell upon me. It was evening when I met her, and the sun was setting up the Brecon Road. I was walking by the almshouses when there came down the steps a tall slight beautiful girl with a graceful figure and long flowing fair hair. Her lovely face was delicately pale, her features refined and aristocratic and her eyes a soft dark tender blue. She looked at me earnestly, longingly and lovingly, and dropped a pretty courtesy. Florence, Florence Hill, sweet Florence Hill, is it you? Once more. Thank God. Once more. My darling, my darling. As she stood and lifted those blue eyes, those soft dark loving eyes shyly to mine, it seemed to me as if the doors and windows of heaven were suddenly opened. It was one of the supreme moments of life. As I stood by the roadside holding her hand, lost to all else and conscious only of her presence, I was in heaven already, or if still on earth in the body, the flights of golden stairs sloped to my feet and one of the angels had come down to me. Florence, Florence Hill, my darling, my darling. It was well nigh all I could say in my emotion. With one long lingering loving look and clasp of the hand we parted and I saw her no more.

THE REVEREND FRANCIS KILVERT
Diary, 23 March 1874 (published 1939)

FIRST LOVE

I NE'ER was struck before that hour
　　With love so sudden and so sweet.
Her face it bloomed like a sweet flower
　　And stole my heart away complete.
My face turned pale as deadly pale,
　　My legs refused to walk away,
And when she looked 'what could I ail?'
　　My life and all seemed turned to clay.

And then my blood rushed to my face
　　And took my sight away.
The trees and bushes round the place
　　Seemed midnight at noonday.
I could not see a single thing,
　　Words from my eyes did start;
They spoke as chords do from the string,
　　And blood burnt round my heart.

Are flowers the winter's choice?
　　Is love's bed always snow?
She seemed to hear my silent voice
　　And love's appeal to know.
I never saw so sweet a face
　　As that I stood before:
My heart has left its dwelling-place
　　And can return no more.

JOHN CLARE
Poems, 1920
(written 1842–64)

POST OFFICE NOTICE.

ST. VALENTINE'S DAY.

LETTERS, LETTER PACKETS, AND PARCELS.

The Public will greatly assist the Post Office by posting their Letters, Parcels, &c., early on **SATURDAY** the **13th FEBRUARY,** in view of the large numbers of Valentines which are sent by post.

It is desirable that Valentines containing, for instance, Cut Flowers, Bouquets, Confectionery, Toys, Fancy Articles, &c., intended for transmission by Parcel Post, should be carefully packed by the Senders so as to secure them from injury during transit.

RATES OF POSTAGE.

For an Inland Letter of any Weight:—	For a Parcel addressed to any part of the United Kingdom:—		These charges
One Penny for the first ounce; a Half-penny for every two ounces additional.	Not exceeding 1 lb. in weight ....3d.		cover the entire service and leave NOTHING TO
	Exceeding 1 lb. and not exceeding 3 lbs. ...6d.		BE PAID by the
	,, 3 lbs. ,, ,, 5 lbs. ...9d.		Addressee on de-
	,, 5 lbs. ,, ,, 7 lbs. ... 1s.		livery.

☞ Parcels intended for transmission by Parcel Post must not be posted in Letter or Newspaper Boxes, but must be handed in at the Counter of a Post Office.

FOREIGN AND COLONIAL PARCELS.

The Foreign and Colonial Parcel Post is in operation to and from Belgium, British Guiana, the Cape of Good Hope, Ceylon, Constantinople, Cyprus, Egypt, Germany, Gibraltar, Grenada, Hong Kong (including certain places in China), India (including Aden and British Burmah), Jamaica, Labuan, the Leeward Islands, Malta, St. Lucia, St. Vincent, the Straits Settlements, Tobago, and Trinidad. The rates for Foreign and Colonial Parcels will be found at pp. 232–3 of the Post Office Guide.

By Command of the Postmaster-General.

GENERAL POST OFFICE,
February, 1886.

Printed for Her Majesty's Stationery Office, by W. P. GRIFFITH & SONS, LIMITED, Prujean Square, Old Bailey, London, E.C.
[111] 120,000

Accept these wishes which your maiden sends,
Ne'er may you feel the want of stedfast friends,
May health, and wealth, and happiness be thine,
And may you welcome this, my Valentine;
Have I another... yes, one wish in store,
That some day we may meet to part no more.

25

VALENTINE, c. 1840

THE LOVE LETTER: WATER-COLOUR BY MARGARET SARAH CARPENTER, *c.* 1840

LOVE LETTER

My dearest Girl, This moment I have set myself to copy some verses out fair. I cannot proceed with any degree of content. I must write you a line or two and see if that will assist in dismissing you from my Mind for ever so short a time. Upon my Soul I can think of nothing else. The time is passed when I had power to advise and warn you against the unpromising morning of my Life. My love has made me selfish. I cannot exist without you. I am forgetful of every thing but seeing you again – my Life seems to stop there – I see no further. You have absorb'd me. I have a sensation at the present moment as though I was dissolving – I should be exquisitely miserable without the hope of soon seeing you. I should be afraid to separate myself far from you. My sweet Fanny, will your heart never change? My love, will it? I have no limit now to my love – Your note came in just here – I cannot be happier away from you. 'Tis richer than an Argosy of Pearles. Do not threat me even in jest. I have been astonished that Men could die Martyrs for religion – I have shudder'd at it. I shudder no more – I could be martyr'd for my Religion – Love is my religion – I could die for that. I could die for you. My Creed is Love and you are its only tenet. You have ravish'd me away by a Power I cannot resist; and yet I could resist till I saw you; and ever since I have seen you I have endeavoured often 'to reason against the reasons of my Love'. I can do that no more – the pain would be too great. My love is selfish. I cannot breathe without you. Yours for ever,

JOHN KEATS, Letter to Fanny Brawne, 1819

ADORATION

AMID the gloom and travail of existence suddenly to behold a beautiful being, and as instantaneously to feel an overwhelming conviction that with that fair form for ever our destiny must be entwined; that there is no more joy than in her joy, no sorrow but when she grieves; that in her sigh of love, in her smile of fondness, hereafter is all bliss; to feel our flaunty ambition fade away like a shrivelled gourd before her vision; to feel fame a juggle and posterity a lie; and to be prepared at once, for this great object, to forfeit and fling away all former hopes, ties, schemes, views; to violate in her favour every duty of society; this is a lover, and this is love. Magnificent, sublime, divine sentiment! An immortal flame burns in the breast of that man who adores and is adored. He is an ethereal being. The accidents of earth touch him not. Revolutions of empire, changes of creed, mutations of opinion, are to him but the clouds and meteors of a stormy sky. The schemes and struggles of mankind are, in his thinking, but the anxieties of pigmies and the fantastical achievements of apes. Nothing can subdue him. He laughs alike at loss of fortune, loss of friends, loss of character. The deeds and thoughts of men are to him equally indifferent. He does not mingle in their paths of callous bustle, or hold himself responsible to the airy impostures before which they bow down. He is a mariner, who, in the sea of life, keeps his gaze fixedly on a single star; and, if that do not shine, he lets go the rudder, and glories when his barque descends into the bottomless gulf.

BENJAMIN DISRAELI, *Henrietta Temple*, 1837

IDOL

DURING the fleeting weeks of that single summer, I lived through my first experience of intense love. All the poetry in my nature centred itself with sudden passion upon a single girl. For me she was the sun and moon, the sea, the hills, and the rivers, the cornfields, the hayfields, the plough-lands, and the first stars of nightfall. Everything that is lovely in nature became illumined by the thought of her: the garden at dawn, as I saw it looking down from the nursery window on the Round-beds and the Crescent-bed, populated with cold, diffident flowers: the meadows by the stream, so hushed in the night air, heavy with the scents of honeysuckle hedges and disturbed only by an occasional deep sighing from one of the ruminating cattle, with weighty body of warm flesh recumbent upon wet summer grass.

From the moment I had seen her in the church I could think of nothing else. My whole approach to life was altered. I no longer cared whether I was to be a poet or not a poet, I no longer was concerned with the deeper problems of existence. Unless I could associate what I saw, heard, tasted, smelt, and touched with her I no longer gave it attention. What reason was there for me to heed the waves that broke day and night against the irregular coasts of the world, to exult in the grass that grew day and night upon the broad back of the stationary land, to watch from ancient elbow-bone bridges the flowing away of rivers, to look up at the crafty midnight stars, unless such appearances could be made to serve in some way as poetical settings for this girl of my utter idolatry? It seemed to me then, as indeed it seems to me still, that every inch of her body shone with some mysterious light . . . that she breathed, that she walked, that she slept to wake again, was an unending source of wonder to me.

LLEWELYN POWYS, *Love and Death*, 1939

GENTLE SHEPHERD, TELL ME WHERE?

TELL me, lovely shepherd, where
Thou feed'st at noon thy fleecy care?
Direct me to the sweet retreat
That guards thee from the mid-day heat:
Lest by the flocks I lonely stray
Without a guide, and lose my way:
Where rest at noon thy bleating care,
Gentle shepherd, tell me where?

EDWARD MOORE, *Poems*, 1756

SHEPHERD AND SHEPHERDESS: ENGLISH NEEDLEWORK PICTURE, EARLY EIGHTEENTH CENTURY

LOVERS: CHELSEA PORCELAIN GROUP, *c.* 1750

BY A BANK OF PINKS AND LILIES

Do not ask me, charming Phillis,
  Why I lead you here alone,
By this bank of pinks and lilies
  And of roses newly blown.

'Tis not to behold the beauty
  Of those flowers that crown the spring;
'Tis to – but I know my duty,
  And dare never name the thing.

('Tis, at worst, but her denying;
  Why should I thus fearful be?
Every minute, gently flying,
  Smiles and says, 'Make use of me.')

What the sun does to those roses,
  While the beams play sweetly in,
I would – but my fear opposes,
  And I dare not name the thing.

Yet I die, if I conceal it;
  Ask my eyes, or ask your own;
And if neither can reveal it,
  Think what lovers think alone.

On this bank of pinks and lilies,
  Might I speak what I would do;
I would with my lovely Phillis –
  I would; I would – Ah! would *you*?

ANONYMOUS
in *The Hive*, 1724

65

ADVICE TO A LOVER...

SILLY boy, 'tis full moon yet, thy night as day shines clearly.
Had thy youth but wit to fear, thou could'st not love so dearly.
Shortly wilt thou mourn, when all thy pleasures are bereaved:
Little knows he how to love that never was deceived.

This is thy first maiden flame, that triumphs yet unstained;
All is artless now you speak; not one word, yet, is feigned;
All is heaven that you behold and all your thoughts are blessëd;
But no Spring can want his Fall, each Troilus hath his Cressid.

Thy well-ordered locks ere long shall rudely hang neglected;
And thy lively pleasant cheer read grief on earth dejected.
Much then wilt thou blame thy Saint, that made thy heart so holy,
And, with sighs, confess, in love, that too much faith is folly.

Yet be just and constant still, Love may beget a wonder,
Not unlike a summer's frost, or winter's fatal thunder.
He that holds his Sweetheart true unto his day of dying
Lives of all that ever breathed most worthy the envying.

THOMAS CAMPION, *The Third Book of Airs, c. 1617*

...AND HIS LASS

Keep, lovely maid, the softness in your eyes,
  To flatter Damon with another day.
When at your feet the ravished lover lies,
  Then put on all that's tender, all that's gay;
And for the grief your absence makes him prove,
Give him the softest, dearest looks of love.

His trembling heart with sweetest smiles caress,
  And in your eyes soft wishes let him find,
That your regret of absence may confess,
  In which no sense of pleasure you could find:
And to restore him, let your faithful eyes
Declare that all his rivals you despise.

APHRA BEHN, *La Montre*, 1686

WITH A GIFT OF A WATCH

WITH me, while present, may thy lovely eyes
    Be never turned upon this golden toy;
Think every pleasing hour too swiftly flies,
    And measure time by joy succeeding joy.

But when the cares that interrupt our bliss
    To me not always will thy sight allow,
Then oft with kind impatience look on this,
    Then every minute count – as I do now.

GEORGE, LORD LYTTELTON
in Dodsley's *Collection of Poems*, 1748
(written *c.* 1732)

EIGHTEENTH·CENTURY WATCH AND CHATELAINE: PHOTOGRAPH BY EDWIN SMITH

THE LACEMAKER: PAINTING BY JAN VERMEER OF DELFT, *c.* 1665

PHILLIS KNOTTING

HEARS not my Phillis how the birds
    Their feathered mates salute?
They tell their passion in their words;
    Must I alone be mute?
      Phillis, without frown or smile,
      Sat and knotted all the while.

The God of Love, in thy bright eyes,
    Does like a tyrant reign;
But in thy heart a child he lies,
    Without his dart or flame.
      Phillis, without frown or smile,
      Sat and knotted all the while.

So many months in silence passed
    (And yet in raging love)
Might well deserve one word, at last,
    My passion should approve.
      Phillis, without frown or smile,
      Sat and knotted all the while.

Must, then, your faithful swain expire,
    And not one look obtain,
Which he, to sooth his fond desire,
    Might pleasingly explain?
      Phillis, without frown or smile,
      Sat and knotted all the while.

SIR CHARLES SEDLEY
in *The Gentleman's Journal*, 1694

LOOK, HOW THE DAFFODILS ARISE

LOOK, how the daffodils arise,
Cheered by the influence of thine eyes,
And others emulating them deny;
   They cannot strain
   To bloom again,
Where such strong beams do fly.

Be not ungrateful, but lie down,
Since for thy sake so brisk they're grown,
And such a downy carpet have bespread,
   That pure delight
   Is freshly dight,
And tricked in white and red.

Be conquered by such charms, there shall
Not always such enticements fall;
What know we, whether that rich spring of light
   Will stanch his streams
   Of golden beams
Ere the approach of night.

How know we whether 't shall not be
The last to either thee or me?
He can at will his ancient brightness gain;
   But thou and I,
   When we shall die,
Shall still in dust remain . . .

JOHN HALL
from 'The Lure', *Poems*, 1646

IN SPRING-TIDE'S GOLDEN HOURS

ALL glorious as a Rainbow's birth
    She came in Spring-tide's golden hours,
When Heaven went hand-in-hand with Earth,
    And May was crowned with buds and flowers.
The mounting devil at my heart
    Clomb faintlier, as my life did win
The charmèd heaven she wrought apart
    To wake its slumbering Angel in.
With radiant mien she trod serene
    And passed me smiling by –
O, who that looked could chance but love?
    Not I, sweet soul, not I.

Her budding breasts, like fragrant fruit,
    Peered out, a-yearning to be pressed:
Her voice shook all my heart's red root,
    Yet might not break a babe's soft rest:
Her being mingled into mine
    As breath of flowers doth mix and melt,
And on her lips a honey-wine
    Was royal-rich as spikenard spilt:
With love a-gush, like water-brooks,
    Her heart smiled in her eye;
O, who that looked could chance but love?
    Not I, sweet soul, not I . . .

GERALD MASSEY
The Ballad of Babe Christabel,
with Other Lyrical Poems, 1854

LOVE ONLY KNOWS PERPETUAL SPRING

Sweet are the charms of her I love,
  More fragrant than the damask rose;
Soft as the down of turtle dove,
  Gentle as wind when zephyr blows;
Refreshing as descending rains
To sun-burnt climes and thirsty plains.

True as the needle to the pole,
  Or as the dial to the sun;
Constant as gliding waters roll,
  Whose swelling tides obey the moon;
From every other charmer free,
My life and love shall follow thee.

The lamb the flowery thyme devours,
  The dam the tender kid pursues;
Sweet Philomel, in shady bowers
  Of verdant spring, her note renews:
All follow what they most admire,
As I pursue my soul's desire.

Nature must change her beauteous face,
  And vary as the seasons rise;
As Winter to the Spring gives place,
  Summer th' approach of Autumn flies:
No change in love the seasons bring,
Love only knows perpetual Spring . . .

BARTON BOOTH
in *The Hive*, 1724

74

MY MISTRESS' FACE

AND would you see my mistress' face?
It is a flowery garden place
Where knots of beauties have such grace
That all is work and nowhere space.

It is a sweet delicious morn
Where day is breeding, never born.
It is a meadow yet unshorn
Whom thousand flowers do adorn.

It is the heavens' bright reflex,
Weak eyes to dazzle and to vex;
It is the Idaea of her sex,
Envy of whom doth world perplex.

It is a face of death that smiles,
Pleasing though it kills the whiles,
Where death and love in pretty wiles
Each other mutually beguiles.

It is fair beauty's freshest youth,
It is the feigned Elysium's truth,
The Spring that wintered hearts reneweth;
And this is that my soul pursueth.

THOMAS CAMPION
in Philip Rosseter's *Book of Airs*, 1601

SWEET AS APRIL SHOWERING

Clear or cloudy, sweet as April showering,
   Smooth or frowning, so is her face to me.
Pleased or smiling, like mild May all flowering,
   When skies blue silk, and meadows carpets be,
Her speeches, notes of that night bird that singeth,
Who, thought all sweet, yet jarring notes out-ringeth.

Her grace like June, when earth and trees be trimmed
   In best attire of complete beauty's height.
Her love again like summer's days be-dimmed
   With little clouds of doubtful constant faith.
Her trust, her doubt, like rain and heat in skies
Gently thundering, she lightning to mine eyes.

Sweet summer-spring, that breatheth life and growing
   In weeds as into herbs and flowers,
And sees of service divers sorts in sowing,
   Some haply seeming, and some being, yours;
Rain on your herbs and flowers that truly serve,
And let your weeds lack dew, and duly starve.

ANONYMOUS
from *The Second Book of Songs or Airs*
composed by John Dowland, 1600

A BEAN FIELD IN BLOSSOM

My love is as sweet as a bean field in blossom;
Like the peabloom her cheek, like the dogrose her bosom:
My love, she's as rich as brook banks of daisies,
Gold eyes and silver rims meeting men's praises;
Her eyes are as bright as the brook's silver ripples,
Milk white are her twin breasts and rose pink the nipples:
Her ankles are sweet as a man can conceive,
And her arms are as fine too though hid in her sleeve.

She's as rosy as morning, as mild as the even;
I sing her love songs, but she's hard of believing:
She'll bid me good day if we meet on the causeway;
If I stop to talk love, in a minute she's saucy:
To kiss or come nigh her there's no use in trying;
She wouldn't touch a man's face though he were dying:
And yet she is lovely as ever was seen,
As the rose o' the wood or pink o' the green.

My love is as sweet as a bean field in blossom;
The snowdrop's not whiter than is her soft bosom:
The plash of the brook it is nothing so bright
As the beams of her eye by bonny moonlight:
The rose o' her cheek no garden so fair
Can match with the red carnations there:
We met where the beanfields were misted wi' dew,
And if she had kissed me why nobody knew.

JOHN CLARE in *The Poet's Eye*
edited by Geoffrey Grigson, 1944
(written *c.* 1840)

WOULD SHE WERE MINE!

. . . HER cheeks are like the blushing cloud
  That beautifies Aurora's face,
Or like the silver crimson shroud
  That Phoebus' smiling looks doth grace;
    Heigh ho, fair Rosalind!
Her lips are like two budded roses
  Whom ranks of lilies neighbour nigh,
Within which bounds she balm encloses,
  Apt to entice a deity:
    Heigh ho, would she were mine!

Her neck like to a stately tower
  Where Love himself imprisoned lies,
To watch for glances every hour
  From her divine and sacred eyes:
    Heigh ho, fair Rosalind!
Her paps are centres of delight,
  Her breasts are orbs of heavenly frame,
Where Nature moulds the dew of light
  To feed perfection with the same;
    Heigh ho, would she were mine! . . .

THOMAS LODGE, *Rosalind*, 1590

BAIGNEUSE: PAINTING BY PIERRE AUGUSTE RENOIR, *c.* 1890

LE PRINTEMPS: SCULPTURE BY AUGUSTE RODIN, 1884

THE GOLDEN MORNING BREAKS

COME away, come, sweet love!
   The golden morning breaks;
All the earth, all the air,
   Of love and pleasure speaks.
Teach thine arms then to embrace,
   And sweet rosy lips to kiss,
   And mix our souls in mutual bliss.
Eyes were made for beauty's grace,
   Viewing, rueing, love-long pain,
   Procured by beauty's rude disdain.

Come away, come, sweet love!
   The golden morning wastes
While the sun from his sphere
   His fiery arrows casts,
Making all the shadows fly,
   Playing, staying in the grove,
   To entertain the stealth of love.
Thither, sweet love, let us hie,
   Flying, dying in desire,
   Winged with sweet hopes and heavenly fire . . .

ANONYMOUS
in *The First Book of Songs or Airs*
composed by John Dowland, 1597

ARE not the joys of morning sweeter
  Than the joys of night?
And are the vigorous joys of youth
  Ashaméd of the light?

Let age and sickness silent rob
  The vineyards in the night;
But those who burn with vigorous youth
  Pluck fruits before the light.

WILLIAM BLAKE, Rossetti MS., 1793

SUMMER

I OFTEN pulled my hat over my eyes to watch the rising of the lark, or to see the hawk hang in the summer sky and the kite take its circles round the wood. I often lingered a minute on the woodland stile to hear the woodpigeons clapping their wings among the dark oaks. I hunted curious flowers in rapture and muttered thoughts in their praise. I loved the pasture with its rushes and thistles and sheep-tracks. I adored the wild, marshy fen with its solitary heronshaw sweeing along in its melancholy sky . . .

I marked the various colours in flat, spreading fields, checkered into closes of different-tinctured grain like the colours of a map; the copper-tinted clover in blossom; the sun-tanned green of the ripening hay; the lighter hues of wheat and barley intermixed with the sunny glare of the yellow charlock and the sunset imitation of the scarlet headaches; the blue cornbottles crowding their splendid colours in large sheets over the land and troubling the cornfields with destroying beauty; the different greens of the woodland trees, the dark oak, the paler ash, the mellow lime, the white poplars peeping above the rest like leafy steeples, the grey willow shining chilly in the sun, as if the morning mist still lingered on its cool green. I loved the meadow lake with its flags and long purples crowding the water's edge. I listened with delight to hear the wind whisper among the feather-topt reeds, to see the taper bulrush nodding in gentle curves to the rippling water; and I watched with delight on haymaking evenings the setting sun drop behind the Brigs and peep again through the half-circle of the arches as if he longed to stay.

JOHN CLARE, quoted in *John Clare*
by J. W. and Anne Tibble, 1932

Now the serpent was more subtle than any beast of the field which the Lord God had made. And he said unto the woman, 'Yea, hath God said ye shall not eat of every tree of the garden?'

And the woman said unto the serpent, 'We may eat of the fruit of the trees of the garden: but of the fruit of the tree which is in the midst of the garden God hath said, "Ye shall not eat of it, neither shall ye touch it, lest ye die."'

And the serpent said unto the woman, 'Ye shall not surely die: for God doth know that in the day ye eat thereof, then your eyes shall be opened, and ye shall be as gods, knowing good and evil.'

And when the woman saw that the tree was good for food, and that it was pleasant to the eyes, and a tree to be desired to make one wise, she took of the fruit thereof, and did eat, and gave also unto her husband with her; and he did eat.

And the eyes of them both were opened, and they knew that they were naked; and they sewed fig leaves together, and made themselves aprons.

And they heard the voice of the Lord God walking in the garden in the cool of the day: and Adam and his wife hid themselves from the presence of the Lord God amongst the trees of the garden.

GENESIS, *Authorized Version*, 1611

ADAM AND EVE: GERMAN STAINED GLASS, EARLY SIXTEENTH CENTURY

THE
ORCHAR...
PAINTI...
BY HEN...
TONKS,
TWENTI...
CENTU...

A BLIND GIRL IN THE ORCHARD

EVERYTHING that could hum, or buzz, or sing, or bloom, had a part in my education—noisy-throated frogs, katydids and crickets held in my hand until, forgetting their embarrassment, they trilled their reedy note, little downy chickens and wildflowers, the dogwood blossoms, meadow-violets and budding fruit trees. I felt the bursting cotton-bolls and fingered their soft fibre and fuzzy seeds; I felt the low soughing of the wind through the cornstalks, the silky rustling of the long leaves, and the indignant snort of my pony, as we caught him in the pasture and put the bit in his mouth—ah me! how well I remember the spicy, clovery smell of his breath!

Sometimes I rose at dawn and stole into the garden while the heavy dew lay on the grass and flowers. Few know what joy it is to feel the roses pressing softly into the hand, or the beautiful motion of the lilies as they sway in the morning breeze. Sometimes I caught an insect in the flower I was plucking, and I felt the faint noise of a pair of wings rubbed together in a sudden terror, as the little creature became aware of a pressure from without.

Another favourite haunt of mine was the orchard, where the fruit ripened early in July. The large, downy peaches would reach themselves into my hand, and as the joyous breezes flew about the trees the apples tumbled at my feet. Oh, the delight with which I gathered up the fruit in my pinafore, pressed my face against the smooth cheeks of the apples, still warm from the sun, and skipped back to the house!

HELEN KELLER, *The Story of My Life*, 1903

BODY...

WHAT lively lad most pleasured me
Of all that with me lay?
I answer that I gave my soul
And loved in misery,
But had great pleasure with a lad
That I loved bodily.

Flinging from his arms I laughed
To think his passion such
He fancied that I gave a soul
Did but our bodies touch,
And laughed upon his breast to think
Beast gave beast as much.

I gave what other women gave
That stepped out of their clothes,
But when this soul, its body off,
Naked to naked goes,
He it has found shall find therein
What none other knows,

And give his own and take his own
And rule in his own right;
And though it loved in misery
Close and cling so tight,
There's not a bird of day that dare
Extinguish that delight.

W. B. YEATS
The Winding Stair and Other Poems, 1933

AND SOUL

O BEAUTY, passing beauty! sweetest Sweet!
   How can'st thou let me waste my youth in sighs?
I only ask to sit beside thy feet.
   Thou knowest I dare not look into thine eyes.
Might I but kiss thy hand! I dare not fold
   My arms about thee – scarcely dare to speak.
And nothing seems to me so wild and bold,
   As with one kiss to touch thy blessed cheek.
Methinks if I should kiss thee, no control
   Within the thrilling brain could keep afloat,
     The subtle spirit. Even while I spoke,
The bare word KISS hath made my inner soul
   To tremble like a lutestring, ere the note
     Hath melted in the silence that it broke.

ALFRED, LORD TENNYSON, *Poems*, 1833

SO SLEEPS MY LOVE

SLEEP, wayward thoughts, and rest you with my love:
  Let not my Love be with my love displeased.
Touch not, proud hands, lest you her anger move,
  But pine you with my longings long diseased.
Thus, while she sleeps, I sorrow for her sake:
So sleeps my Love, and yet my love doth wake.

But O the fury of my restless fear!
  The hidden anguish of my flesh desires!
The glories and the beauties that appear
  Between her brows, near Cupid's closèd fires!
Thus, while she sleeps, moves sighing for her sake:
So sleeps my Love, and yet my love doth wake.

My love doth rage, and yet my Love doth rest:
  Fear in my love, and yet my Love secure;
Peace in my Love, and yet my love oppressed,
  Impatient yet of perfect temperature.
Sleep, dainty Love, while I sigh for thy sake:
So sleeps my Love, and yet my love doth wake.

ANONYMOUS, in *The First Book of Songs or Airs*
composed by John Dowland, 1597

HAYMAKER AND SLEEPING GIRL: PAINTING BY THOMAS GAINSBOROUGH, R.A., *c.* 1786

LE BAISER DONNÉ: SÈVRES PORCELAIN GROUP BY FALCONET, 1765

I PRESSED HER REBEL LIPS

I GENTLY touched her hand: she gave
A look that did my soul enslave;
I pressed her rebel lips in vain:
They rose up to be pressed again.
  Thus happy, I no farther meant,
  Than to be pleased and innocent.

On her soft breasts my hand I laid,
And a quick, light impression made;
They with a kindly warmth did glow,
And swelled, and seemed to over-flow.
  Yet, trust me, I no farther meant,
  Than to be pleased and innocent.

On her eyes my eyes did stay:
O'er her smooth limbs my hands did stray;
Each sense was ravished with delight,
And my soul stood prepared for flight.
  Blame me not if at last I meant
  More to be pleased than innocent.

ANONYMOUS
in *Mercurius Musicus*, 1699

UNDER THE WILLOW SHADES

UNDER the willow shades they were
   Free from the eye-sight of the sun,
For no intruding beam could there
   Peep through to spy what things were done:
     Thus sheltered, they unseen did lie,
     Surfeiting on each other's eye;
Defended by the willow shades alone,
The sun's heat they defied, and cooled their own.

Whilst they did embrace unspied,
   The conscious willows seemed to smile,
That they with privacy supplied,
   Holding the door, as 'twere, the while,
     And, when their dalliances were o'er,
     The willows, to oblige 'em more,
Bowing, did seem to say, as they withdrew,
'We can supply you with a cradle, too.'

SIR WILLIAM DAVENANT
The Rivals, 1668

ADDRESS TO A NIGHTINGALE

WHILE in the bower, with beauty blest,
    The loved Amintor lies;
While sinking on Zelinda's breast,
    He fondly kissed her eyes;

A wakeful nightingale, who long
    Had mourned within the shade,
Sweetly renewed her plaintive song,
    And warbled thro' the glade.

'Melodious songstress,' cried the Swain,
    'To shades less happy go;
Or, if with us thou wilt remain,
    Forbear thy tuneful woe.

'While in Zelinda's arms I lie,
    To song I am not free;
On her soft bosom while I sigh,
    I discord find in thee.

'Zelinda gives me perfect joys:
    Then cease thy fond intrusion;
Be silent; music now is noise,
    Variety confusion.'

LEONARD WELSTED
Epistles, Odes, &c., 1724

LOVE PLAY

SWEET, let us love enjoy,
And play and tick and toy,
And all our cares will drown:
Smile, laugh, and sometimes frown,
Make love's parenthesis
With a sweet, melting kiss.

Then whisper in each ear,
Love's pretty tales to hear;
If wanton, cry 'Oh, man!'
And strike me with your fan;
If offer thee to dandle,
Then rap me with the handle.

For all this, I'll not miss
Thy lips, but steal a kiss;
Cause it is stolen, then
I'll give it you again,
Play with your little hand,
And kiss it as I stand.

Then, though you think it much,
We'll one another touch,
As carelessly, not knowing
How love is now a-growing,
As if you did not mind it –
Yet both of us will find it . . .

WILLIAM CAVENDISH, MARQUIS OF
NEWCASTLE, *The Phanseys*, 1645

NEST OF JOY

As burnished gold, such are my Sovereign's hairs;
   A brace of stars divine her blackish eyes,
Like to the fairest black the raven bears,
   Or fairer, if you fairer can devise:
So likewise fair's the beauty of her breasts,
Where pleasure lurks, where joy still dallying rests.

This Venus' bower you rightly may compare
   To whitest snow that e'er from heaven fell,
Or to the mines of alabaster fair.
   Woe's me! 'Tis sweet to sleep in Cupid's cell,
Whilst he the heart makes surfeit with delight
Through golden hair, black eyes, and breast most white.

ROBERT TOFTE, *Laura*, 1597

A GIFT OF ROSES

Go, lovely pair of roses, go,
   This clad in scarlet, that in snow.
Go, say to my ungentle fair,
   (If on your forms she deigns to gaze)
You dare not hope to rival her,
   Or match the glories of her face;
But that you're humbly sent to prove
A youth undone by beauty and her love.

The sickly white in this pale rose
My wan and meagre looks disclose;
But that which shines so fiercely bright,
   Whose head in painted flames aspires,
And blushes so with purple light,
   It seems to send forth real fires,
Tell her that rose's ruddy fires impart
The flames her eyes have kindled in my heart.

JOHN SMITH
Poems Upon Several Occasions, 1713

LILY OF THE VALE

THE fragrant Lily of the Vale,
    So elegantly fair,
Whose sweets perfume the fanning gale,
    To Chloe I compare.

What tho' on earth it lowly grows
    And strives its head to hide;
Its sweetness far out-vies the Rose,
    That flaunts with so much pride.

The costly Tulip owes its hue
    To many a gaudy stain;
In this, we view the virgin white
    Of innocence remain.

See how the curious Florist's hand
    Uprears its humble head;
And to preserve the charming flower,
    Transplants it to his bed.

There, while it sheds its sweets around,
    How shines each modest grace!
Enraptured how its owner stands,
    To view its lovely face!

But pray, my Chloe, now observe
    The inference of my tale;
May I the Florist be – and thou
    The Lily of the Vale.

ANONYMOUS
in *The Bull-Finch, c.* 1780

A BROKEN-HEARTED GARDENER

I'M a broken-hearted Gardener, and don't know what to do,
My love she is inconstant, and a fickle jade, too,
One smile from her lips will never be forgot,
It refreshes, like a shower from a watering pot.

CHORUS: *Oh, Oh! she's a fickle wild rose,*
        A damask, a cabbage, a young China Rose.

She's my myrtle, my geranium,
My Sun flower, my sweet marjorum.
My honey suckle, my tulip, my violet,
My holy hock, my dahlia, my mignonette.

We grew up together like two apple trees,
And clung to each other like double sweet peas,
Now they're going to trim her, and plant her in a pot,
And I'm left to wither, neglected and forgot.

She's my snowdrop, my ranunculus,
My hyacinth, my gilliflower, my polyanthus,
My heart's ease, my pink water lily,
My buttercup, my daisy, my daffydown dilly.

I'm like a scarlet runner that has lost its stick,
Or a cherry that's left for the dickey to pick,
Like a waterpot I weep, like a paviour I sigh,
Like a mushroom I'll wither, like a cucumber, die . . .

VICTORIAN STREET BALLAD
in *Modern Street Ballads*, edited by John Ashton, 1888

A GARDENER: NINETEENTH-CENTURY COLOURED WAX

FLOWER PIECE

My lady's presence makes the roses red,
  Because to see her lips they blush for shame.
  The lily's leaves, for envy, pale became,
And her white hands in them this envy bred.
The marigold the leaves abroad did spread,
  Because the sun's and her power is the same.
  The violet of purple colour came,
Dyed in the blood she made my heart to shed.
In brief, all flowers from her their virtue take;
  From her sweet breath their sweet smells do proceed;
The living heat which her eyebeams doth make
  Warmeth the ground, and quickeneth the seed.
The rain, wherewith she watereth the flowers,
Falls from mine eyes, which she dissolves in showers.

HENRY CONSTABLE, *Diana*, 1594

FLOWER PIECE:
PAINTING
BY NICHOLAS
VAN VERENDAEL,
SEVENTEENTH
CENTURY

MY LOVE IS LIKE A RED RED ROSE

My love is like a red red rose
   That's newly sprung in June:
My love is like the melody
   That's sweetly play'd in tune.

As fair art thou, my bonnie lass,
   So deep in love am I:
And I will love thee still, my dear,
   Till a' the seas gang dry.

Till a' the seas gang dry, my dear,
   And the rocks melt wi' the sun:
And I will love thee still, my dear,
   While the sands o' life shall run.

And fare thee weel, my only love,
   And fare thee weel a while!
And I will come again, my love,
   Tho' it were ten thousand mile.

ROBERT BURNS
in *A Selection of Scots Songs*, II, 1794

THE MEANING OF THE ROSE

YE shall also find this written of roses, that at the first they were all white, and that they became red afterward with the blood of the Goddess Venus, which was done in this sort. Venus loved the younker Adonis better than the warrior Mars (who loved Venus with all his force and might) but when Mars perceived that Venus loved Adonis better than him, he slew Adonis, thinking by this means to cause Venus not only to forgo, but also to forget, her friend Adonis, and so to love Mars only; of the which thing, when Venus had warning how and where it should be accomplished, she was suddenly moved and hastily ran to have rescued Adonis, but taking no care of the way, at a sudden, ere she was aware, she threw herself upon a bed or thicket of white roses, where as with sharp cruel thorns, her tender feet were so pricked and wounded, that the blood sprang out abundantly, wherewithal when the roses were bedewed and sprinkled, they became all red, the which colour they do yet keep, more or less, according to the quantity of the blood that fell upon them, in remembrance of the clear and pleasant Venus. Some others write that for very anger which she had conceived against Mars for the killing of her friend, the fair Adonis, she gave her tender body willingly to be spoiled and mangled, and, in despite of Mars, she threw herself into a bed or arbour of prickly roses.

Some say also that Roses became red, with the casting down of that heavenly drink Nectar, which was used by Cupid, that wanton boy, who, playing with the Gods sitting at a banquet, with his wings overthrew the pot wherein the Nectar was. As therefore as Philostratus saith, the rose is the flower of Cupid, or Cupid's flower.

REMBERT DODOENS, *A New Herbal, or History of Plants*
translated by Henry Lyte, 1578

LOVE MAKES THEM DANCE

What makes the vine about the elm to dance
   With turnings, windings, and embracements round?
What makes the lodestone to the north advance
   His subtle point, as if from thence he found
   His chief attractive virtue to redound?
Kind nature first doth cause all things to love;
Love makes them dance, and in just order move . . .

Thus when at first Love had them marshallèd,
   As erst he did the shapeless mass of things,
He taught them rounds and winding *hays* to tread,
   And about trees to cast themselves in rings;
   As the two Bears, whom the first mover flings
With a short turn about heav'n's axle-tree,
In a round dance for ever wheeling be . . .

Thus Love taught men, and men thus learned of Love
   Sweet music's sound with feet to counterfeit;
Which was long time before high-thundering Jove
   Was lifted up to heaven's imperial seat;
   For though by birth he were the prince of Crete
Nor Crete nor heaven should that young prince have seen
   If dancers with their timbrels had not been . . .

SIR JOHN DAVIES
Orchestra, or A Poem of Dancing, 1596

DANCERS: PREHISTORIC ROCK PAINTING, HOGGAR MOUNTAINS, SAHARA

DANCERS: MEISSEN PORCELAIN GROUP BY J. F. EBERLEIN, *c.* 1735

PERILS OF THE DANCE

DANCING is for the most part attended with many amorous smiles, wanton compliments, unchaste kisses, scurrilous songs and sonnets, effeminate music, lust-provoking attire, ridiculous love-pranks; all which savour only of sensuality, of raging fleshly lusts. Therefore it is wholly to be abandoned of all good Christians. Dancing serves no necessary use, no profitable, laudable, or pious end at all; it issues only from the inbred pravity, vanity, wantonness, incontinency, pride, profaneness, or madness of men's depraved natures. Therefore it must needs be unlawful unto Christians. The way to heaven is too steep, too narrow, for men to dance in and keep revel-rout: No way is large or smooth enough for capering roisters, for jumping, skipping, dancing dames, but that broad, beaten, pleasant road that leads to hell.

WILLIAM PRYNNE, *Histriomastix*, 1633

AFTER THE BALL

Come into the garden, Maud,
  For the black bat, night, has flown,
Come into the garden, Maud,
  I am here at the gate alone;
And the woodbine spices are wafted abroad,
  And the musk of the rose is blown.

For a breeze of morning moves,
  And the planet of Love is on high,
Beginning to faint in the light that she loves
  On a bed of daffodil sky,
To faint in the light of the sun she loves,
  To faint in his light, and to die.

All night have the roses heard
  The flute, violin, bassoon;
All night has the casement jessamine stirr'd
  To the dancers dancing in tune;
Till a silence fell with the waking bird,
  And a hush with the setting moon.

I said to the lily, 'There is but one
  With whom she has heart to be gay.
When will the dancers leave her alone?
  She is weary of dance and play.'
Now half to the setting moon are gone,
  And half to the rising day;
Low on the sand and loud on the stone
  The last wheel echoes away.

I said to the rose, 'The brief night goes
   In babble and revel and wine.
O young lord-lover, what sighs are those
   For one that will never be thine?
But mine, but mine,' so I sware to the rose,
   'For ever and ever, mine.'

And the soul of the rose went into my blood,
   As the music clash'd in the hall;
And long by the garden lake I stood,
   For I heard your rivulet fall
From the lake to the meadow and on to the wood,
   Our wood, that is dearer than all . . .

Queen rose of the rosebud garden of girls,
   Come hither, the dances are done,
In gloss of satin and glimmer of pearls,
   Queen lily and rose in one;
Shine out, little head, sunning over with curls,
   To the flowers, and be their sun.

There has fallen a splendid tear
   From the passion-flower at the gate.
She is coming, my dove, my dear;
   She is coming, my life, my fate;
The red rose cries, 'She is near, she is near;'
   And the white rose weeps, 'She is late;'
The larkspur listens, 'I hear, I hear;'
   And the lily whispers, 'I wait . . .'

ALFRED, LORD TENNYSON
Maud, and Other Poems, 1855

III

I CANNOT DANCE TONIGHT

Oʜ! when they brought me hither, they wonder'd at my wild
   delight,
But would I were at home again, I cannot dance to-night!
How can they all look so cheerful? the dance seems strangely dull
   to me;
The music sounds so mournful, what can the reason be?
   Oh! when they brought me hither, they wonder'd at my wild delight,
   But would I were at home again, I cannot dance to-night!

Hark! Hark! at length he's coming, I'm not weary – let me stay!
I hear his laugh distinctly now, 'twill chase the gloom away.
Oh! would that I were near him, he sees me not amid the crowd,
He hears me not – ah! would I dared to breathe his name aloud.
   Oh! when they brought me hither, they wonder'd at my wild delight,
   But would I were at home again, I cannot dance to-night!

He leaves that group of triflers, and with the smile I love to see,
He seems to seek for some one – oh! is it not for me?
No, no! 'tis for that dark-eyed girl, I see her now return his glance,
He passes me, he takes her hand, he leads her to the dance!
   Oh! when they brought me hither, they wonder'd at my wild delight,
   But would I were at home again, I cannot dance to-night!

THOMAS HAYNES BAYLY
Songs, Ballads and Other Poems, 1857

BALLROOM GOWNS: HAND-COLOURED FASHION PLATE AFTER ADÈLE ANAIS TOUDOUZE, 1853

'DANCE, LITTLE LADY!' LAURI DEVINE IN THE ORIGINAL PRODUCTION, 1928

DANCE, LITTLE LADY!

DANCE, dance, dance, little lady!
Youth is fleeting
To the rhythm beating
  In your mind.
Dance, dance, dance, little lady!
So obsessed
With second-best, no rest
  You'll ever find.
Time and tide and trouble
Never, never wait;
Let the cauldron bubble,
Justify your fate.
Dance, dance, dance, little lady!
Dance, dance, dance, little lady!
  Leave tomorrow behind.

NOËL COWARD
in *This Year of Grace*, 1928

HOPING THIS FINDS YOU WELL

DEAR ALF, I seen you last night in my dream. O my dear I cried at waking up. What a silly girl you been and got. The pain is bad this morning but I laugh at the sollum cloks of the sisters and the saw-bones. I can see they think I am booked but they don't know what has befalen between you and me. How could I die and leave my Dear. I spill my medecin this morning thinking of my Dear. Hoping this finds you well no more now from yours truly, Liz.

ANONYMOUS, quoted from a newspaper report
in *Love* by Walter de la Mare, 1943

BROKEN VOWS

IT is late last night the dog was speaking of you; the snipe was speaking of you in her deep marsh. It is you are the lonely bird throughout the woods; and that you may be without a mate until you find me.

You promised me and you said a lie to me, that you would be before me where the sheep are flocked. I gave a whistle and three hundred cries to you; and I found nothing there but a bleating lamb.

You promised me a thing that was hard for you, a ship of gold under a silver mast; twelve towns and a market in all of them, and a fine white court by the side of the sea.

You promised me a thing that is not possible; that you would give me gloves of the skin of a fish; that you would give me shoes of the skin of a bird, and a suit of the dearest silk in Ireland.

My mother said to me not to be talking with you, to-day or to-morrow or on Sunday. It was a bad time she took for telling me that, it was shutting the door after the house was robbed.

You have taken the east from me, you have taken the west from me, you have taken what is before me and what is behind me; you have taken the moon, you have taken the sun from me, and my fear is great you have taken God from me.

ANONYMOUS, quoted in *Ideas of Good and Evil*
by W. B. Yeats, 1903

SECRET LOVE

I FEED a flame within, which so torments me
That it both pains my heart, and yet contents me:
'Tis such a pleasing smart, and I so love it,
That I had rather die than once remove it.

Yet he for whom I grieve shall never know it;
My tongue does not betray, nor my eyes show it.
Not a sigh, nor a tear, my pain discloses,
But they fall silently, like dew on roses.

Thus, to prevent my Love from being cruel,
My heart's the sacrifice, as 'tis the fuel;
And while I suffer this to give him quiet,
My faith rewards my love, though he deny it.

On his eyes will I gaze, and there delight me;
While I conceal my love no frown can fright me.
To be more happy I dare not aspire,
Nor can I fall more low, mounting no higher.

JOHN DRYDEN, *Secret-Love, or*
The Maiden Queen, 1668

FATAL LOVE

WHY do I love? Go, ask the glorious sun
Why every day it round the world doth run;
Ask Thames and Tiber why they ebb and flow;
Ask damask roses why in June they blow;
Ask ice and hail the reason why they're cold;
Decaying beauties, why they will grow old.
They'll tell thee Fate, that every thing doth move,
Enforces them to this, and me to love.
There is no reason for our love or hate;
'Tis irresistible, as death or fate.
'Tis not his face; I've sense enough to see
That is not good, though doated on by me;
Not is't his tongue that has this conquest won,
For that at least is equalled by my own:
His carriage can to none obliging be;
'Tis rude, affected, full of vanity,
Strangely ill-natured, peevish and unkind,
Unconstant, false, to jealousy inclined:
His temper could not have so great a power;
'Tis mutable, and changes every hour:
Those vigorous years that women so adore
Are past in him; he's twice my age, and more.
And yet I love this false, this worthless man
With all the passion that a woman can;
Doat on his imperfections; though I spy
Nothing to love, I love, and know not why:
Since 'tis decreed in the dark book of fate
That I should love and he should be ingrate.

'EPHELIA', *Female Poems on Several Occasions*, 1679

TEARS

STAY, pretty prodigal, oh stay;
Throw not those pearly drops away;
Each little shining gem might be
Price for a captive prince's liberty:
See down her cheeks the shining jewels slide,
Brighter than meteors that from heaven do glide.

Sorrow n'er looked before so fair,
Nor ever had so sweet an air:
All-conquering rays her woes do dart,
And unknown passions to the soul impart:
More fair she looks, while grief her face doth shroud,
Than the sun peeping through a watery cloud.

Oh, turn away those killing eyes!
Venus from such a sea did rise:
Love doth in tears triumphant ride;
Such mighty charms can never be denied:
That at one sight such different passions move,
Relenting pity, and commanding love.

Come, curious artist, as they fall,
Gather the shining jewels all;
Harden the gems, and each will be
More valued than the Indies' treasury:
But, if the secret doth exceed thy art,
It is but borrowing hardness from her heart.

THOMAS HEYRICK, *Miscellany Poems*, 1691

AND KISSES

COME hither, womankind and all their worth,
Give me thy kisses as I call them forth.
Give me the billing kiss, that of the dove,
    A kiss of love;
The melting kiss, a kiss that doth consume
    To a perfume;
The extract kiss, of every sweet a part,
    A kiss of art;
The kiss which ever stirs some new delight,
    A kiss of might;
The twaching smacking kiss, and when you cease,
    A kiss of peace;
The music kiss, crochet-and-quaver time;
    The kiss of rhyme;
The kiss of eloquence, which doth belong
    Unto the tongue;
The kiss of all the sciences in one,
    The Kiss alone.
So, 'tis enough.

EDWARD, LORD HERBERT OF CHERBURY
Occasional Verses, 1665 (written *c.* 1620)

BETWEEN TWO FIRES

How happy could I be with either,
  Were t'other dear charmer away!
But while you thus teaze me together,
  To neither a word will I say;

But tol-de-rol, lol-de-rol-laddie
Te-rol-de-rol, lol-de-rol-ay!
But tol-de-rol, lol-de-rol-laddie
Te-rol-de-rol, lol-de-rol-ay!

JOHN GAY, *The Beggar's Opera*, 1728

STAFFORDSHIRE POTTERY SALTGLAZE PEW GROUP, *c.* 1730

CARD PLAYERS: PAINTING BY NICOLAS MAES, MID SEVENTEENTH CENTURY

A WAITING GAME

FAIR Celia she is nice and coy,
  While she holds the lucky lure;
Her repartees are *Pish!* and *Fie!*
  And you in vain pursue her.

Stay but 'till her hand be out,
  And she become your debtor;
Address her then, and, without doubt,
  You'll speed a great deal better . . .

ANONYMOUS
in *The Hive*, 1724

CALL HOME THE HEART

I PRAY thee leave, love me no more,
   Call home the heart you gave me!
I but in vain that saint adore
   That can but will not save me.
These poor half-kisses kill me quite;
   Was ever man thus servëd,
Amidst an ocean of delight
   For pleasure to be starvëd?

Show me no more those snowy breasts
   With azure riverets branchëd,
Where, whilst mine eye with plenty feasts,
   Yet is my thirst not stanchëd.
O Tantalus, thy pains ne'er tell!
   By me thou art prevented:
'Tis nothing to be plagued in Hell,
   But thus in Heaven tormented!

Clip me no more in those dear arms,
   Nor thy life's comfort call me!
O these are but too powerful charms,
   And do but more enthral me.
But see, how patient I am grown
   In all this coil about thee!
Come, nice thing, let thy heart alone!
   I cannot live without thee.

MICHAEL DRAYTON
Odes, with Other Lyric Poesies, 1619

THE CHANGELESS IMAGE

HATE me or love, I care not, as I pass
To those hid citadels
Where in the depth of my enchanted glass
The changeless image dwells;
To where for ever blooms the nameless tree;
For ever, alone and fair,
The lovely Unicorn beside the sea
Is laid, and slumbers there.

Give or withhold, all's nothing, as I go
On to those glimmering grounds
Where falling secretly and quiet as snow
The silent music sounds;
Where earth is withered away before the eyes,
And heaven hangs in the air,
For in the oak the bird of paradise
Alights, and triumphs there.

Slay me or spare, it matters not: I fly
Ever, for ever rest
Alone and with a host: in the void sky
There do I build my nest:
I lay my beams from star to star, and make
My house where all is bare;
Hate, slay, withhold, I rear it for thy sake
And thou art with me there.

RUTH PITTER
A Trophy of Arms, 1936

A LEAVE-TAKING

LET us go hence, my songs; she will not hear.
Let us go hence together without fear;
Keep silence now, for singing-time is over,
And over all old things and all things dear.
She loves not you nor me as all we love her.
Yea, though we sang as angels in her ear,
  She would not hear . . .

Let us go home and hence; she will not weep.
We gave love many dreams and days to keep,
Flowers without scent, and fruits that would not grow,
Saying 'If thou wilt, thrust in thy sickle and reap.'
All is reaped now; no grass is left to mow;
And we that sowed, though all we fell on sleep,
  She would not weep.

Let us go hence and rest; she will not love.
She shall not hear us if we sing hereof,
Nor see love's ways, how sore they are and steep.
Come hence, let be, lie still; it is enough.
Love is a barren sea, bitter and deep;
And though she saw all heaven in flower above,
  She would not love . . .

ALGERNON CHARLES SWINBURNE
Poems and Ballads, 1866

MAN PLAYING A HURDY-GURDY: PAINTING BY JEAN ANTOINE WATTEAU, EIGHTEENTH CENTURY

A LADY OF THE LAKE FAMILY: DETAIL OF PAINTING BY SIR PETER LELY, *c.* 1660

SYREN SONG

You that think Love can convey
No other way
But through the eyes, into the heart,
His fatal dart,
Close up those casements, and but hear
This syren sing;
And on the wing
Of her sweet voice it shall appear,
That Love can enter at the ear.

Then unveil your eyes; behold
The curious mould
Where that voice dwells; and, as we know,
When the cocks crow
And Sol is mounted on his way,
We freely may
Gaze on the day;
So may you, when the music's done,
Awake, and see the rising sun.

THOMAS CAREW, *Poems*, 1640

THE DAYLONG VOICE

HE would declare and could himself believe
    That the birds there in all the garden round
From having heard the daylong voice of Eve
    Had added to their own an oversound,
Her tone of meaning but without the words.
    Admittedly an eloquence so soft
Could only have had an influence on birds
    When call or laughter carried it aloft.
Be that as may be, she was in their song.
    Moreover her voice upon their voices crossed
Had now persisted in the woods so long
    That probably it never would be lost.
Never again would birds' song be the same.
And to do that to birds was why she came.

ROBERT FROST, *A Witness Tree*, 1943

THE SILENT VOICE

Love hath a language of his own –
   A voice that goes
From heart to heart – whose mystic tone
   Love only knows.

The lotus-flower, whose leaves I now
   Kiss silently,
Far more than words will tell thee how
   I worship thee.

The mirror, which to thee I hold, –
   Which, when impressed
With thy bright looks, I turn and fold
   To this fond breast –

Doth it not speak, beyond all spells
   Of poet's art,
How deep thy hidden image dwells
   In this hushed heart?

THOMAS MOORE (from the Persian)
in *The Tribute*, 1837

MOURN BOLDLY, MY INK

MOST blessed paper, which shalt kiss that hand whereto all blessed-ness is in nature a servant, do not yet disdain to carry with thee the woeful words of a miser now despairing; neither be afraid to appear before her, bearing the base title of the sender; for no sooner shall that divine hand touch thee but that thy baseness shall be turned to most high preferment. Therefore mourn boldly, my ink; for while she looks upon you your blackness will shine: cry out boldly, my lamentation, for while she reads you your cries will be music.

SIR PHILIP SIDNEY, *Arcadia*, 1590

THE LETTER READER: PAINTING BY GABRIEL METSU, MID SEVENTEENTH CENTURY

ENGRAVED SILVER TAZZA: LONDON 1688

CONTRACT OF MARRIAGE

(*Enter Millament and Mirabell.*)

Mir. 'Like Daphne she, as lovely and as coy.' Do you lock yourself up from me, to make my search more curious? or is this pretty artifice contrived to signify that here the chase must end, and my pursuits be crowned? For you can fly no further.

Mil. Vanity! no – I'll fly, and be followed to the last moment. Though I am upon the very verge of matrimony, I expect you should solicit me as much as if I were wavering at the grate of a monastery, with one foot over the threshold. I'll be solicited to the very last, nay, and afterwards.

Mir. What, after the last?

Mil. Oh, I should think I was poor and had nothing to bestow, if I were reduced to an inglorious ease, and freed from the agreeable fatigues of solicitation.

Mir. But do not you know, that when favours are conferred upon instant and tedious solicitation, that they diminish in their value, and that both the giver loses the grace, and the receiver lessens his pleasure?

Mil. It may be in things of common application; but never sure in love. Oh, I hate a lover that can dare to think he draws a moment's air, independent on the bounty of his mistress. There is not so impudent a thing in nature, as the saucy look of an assured man, confident of success. The pedantic arrogance of a very husband has not so pragmatical an air. Ah! I'll never marry, unless I am first made sure of my will and pleasure.

Mir. Would you have 'em both before marriage? or will you be contented with the first now, and stay for the other till after grace?

Mil. Ah! don't be impertinent. – My dear liberty, shall I leave thee? my faithful solitude, my darling contemplation, must I bid you then adieu? Ay-h adieu – my morning thoughts, agreeable wakings, indolent slumbers, all ye *douceurs*, ye *sommeils du matin*, *adieu*? – I can't do't, 'tis more than impossible – positively, Mirabell, I'll lie abed in a morning as long as I please.

Mir. Then I'll get up in a morning as early as I please.

Mil. Ah! idle creature, get up when you will – and d'ye hear, I won't be called names after I'm married; positively I won't be called names.

Mir. Names!

Mil. Ay, as Wife, Spouse, My Dear, Joy, Jewel, Love, Sweetheart, and the rest of that nauseous cant, in which men and their wives are so fulsomely familiar – I shall never bear that – good Mirabell, don't let us be familiar or fond, nor kiss before folks, like my lady Fadler, and Sir Francis: nor go to Hide-park together the first Sunday in a new chariot, to provoke eyes and whispers, and then never be seen there together again; as if we were proud of one another the first week, and ashamed of one another ever after. Let us never visit together nor go to a play together; but let us be very strange and well-bred: let us be as strange as if we had been married a great while; and as well bred as if we were not married at all.

Mir. Have you any more conditions to offer? Hitherto your demands are pretty reasonable.

Mil. Trifles! – As liberty to pay and receive visits to and from whom I please; to write and receive letters, without interrogatories or wry faces on your part; to wear what I please; and choose conversation with regard only to my own taste; to have no obligation upon me to converse with wits that I don't like, because they are your acquaintance; or to be intimate with fools, because they may be your relations. Come to dinner when I please; dine in my dressing-room when I'm out of humour, without giving a reason. To have my closet inviolate; to be sole empress of my tea-table, which you must never presume to approach without first asking leave. And, lastly, wherever I am, you shall always knock at the door before you come in. These articles subscribed, if I continue to endure you a little longer, I may by degrees dwindle into a wife.

Mir. Your bill of fare is something advanced in this latter account. Well, have I liberty to offer conditions – that when you are dwindled into a wife, I may not be beyond measure enlarged into a husband?

Mil. You have free leave; propose your utmost, speak and spare not.

Mir. I thank you. *Inprimis* then, I covenant, that your acquaintance be general; that you admit no sworn confidant, or intimate of your own sex; no she friend to screen her affairs under your countenance, and tempt you to make trial of a mutual secrecy. No decoy duck to wheedle you a fop-scrambling to the play in a mask – then bring you home in a pretended fright, when you think you shall be found out – and rail at me for missing the play, and disappointing the frolic which you had to pick me up, and prove my constancy.

Mil. Detestable *inprimis*! I go to the play in a mask!

Mir. Item, I article, that you continue to like your own face, as long as I shall: and while it passes current with me, that you endeavour not to new-coin it. To which end, together with all vizards for the day, I prohibit all masks for the night, made of oiled-skins, and I know not what – hogs' bones, hares' gall, pig-water, and the marrow of a roasted cat. In short, I forbid all commerce with the gentlewoman in what-d'ye-call-it Court. Item, I shut my doors against all bawds with baskets, and penny-worths of muslin, china, fans, atlasses, etc. Item, when you shall be breeding –

Mil. Ah! name it not.

Mir. Which may be presumed with a blessing on our endeavours –

Mil. Odious endeavours!

Mir. I denounce against all strait lacing, squeezing for a shape, till you mould my boy's head like a sugar-loaf, and instead of a man-child, make me father to a crooked billet. Lastly, to the dominion of the tea-table I submit – but with proviso, that you exceed not in your province; but restrain yourself to native and simple tea-table drinks, as tea, chocolate, and coffee: as likewise to genuine and authorized tea-table talk – such as mending of fashions, spoiling reputations, railing at absent friends, and so forth – but that on no account you encroach upon the men's prerogative, and presume to drink healths, or toast fellows; for prevention of which I banish all foreign forces, all auxiliaries to the tea-table, as orange-brandy, all aniseed, cinnamon, citron and Barbadoes-waters, together with ratafia, and the most noble spirit of clary – but for cowslip wine, poppy water, and all dormitives, those I allow – These provisos admitted, in other things I may prove a tractable and complying husband.

Mil. O horrid provisos! filthy strong-waters! I toast fellows! odious men! I hate your odious provisos.

Mir. Then we are agreed! shall I kiss your hand upon the contract?

WILLIAM CONGREVE, *The Way of the World*, 1700

BY the time you say you're his,
  Shivering and sighing,
And he vows his passion is
  Infinite, undying –
Lady, make a note of this,
  One of you is lying.

DOROTHY PARKER
Not So Deep as a Well, 1937

REFLECTIONS

THERE are two births; the one when light
  First strikes the new awakened sense;
The other when two souls unite,
  And we must count our life from thence:
When you loved me and I loved you
Then both of us were born anew . . .

WILLIAM CARTWRIGHT,
Plays and Poems, 1651 (written *c.* 1636)

LOVE wakes men, once a life-time each;
  They lift their heavy lids, and look;
And lo, what one sweet page can teach,
  They read with joy, then shut the book.
And some give thanks, and some blaspheme,
  And most forget; but, either way,
That and the Child's unheeded dream
  Is all the light of all their day.

COVENTRY PATMORE
The Angel in the House, 1862

SOME kill their love when they are young,
  And some when they are old;
Some strangle with the hands of Lust,
  Some with the hands of Gold:
The kindest use a knife, because
  The dead so soon grow cold . . .

OSCAR WILDE
The Ballad of Reading Gaol, 1898

WEDDING MORN

THE morning breaks like a pomegranate
    In a shining crack of red;
Ah, when tomorrow the dawn comes late
    Whitening across the bed
It will find me watching at the marriage gate
    And waiting while light is shed
On him who is sleeping satiate
    With a sunk, unconscious head.

And when the dawn comes creeping in,
    Cautiously I shall raise
Myself to watch the daylight win
    On my first of days,
As it shows him sleeping a sleep he got
    With me, as under my gaze
He grows distinct, and I see his hot
    Face freed of the wavering blaze.

Then I shall know which image of God
    My man is made toward;
And I shall see my sleeping rod
    Or my life's reward;
And I shall count the stamp and worth
    Of the man I've accepted as mine,
Shall see an image of heaven or of earth
    On his minted metal shine.

Oh, and I long to see him sleep
    In my power utterly;
So I shall know what I have to keep.
    I long to see
My love, that spinning coin, laid still
    And plain at the side of me
For me to reckon – for surely he will
    Be wealth of life to me.

And then he will be mine, he will lie
    Revealed to me;
Patent and open beneath my eye
    He will sleep of me;
He will lie negligent, resign
    His truth to me, and I
Shall watch the dawn light up for me
    This fate of mine.

And as I watch the wan light shine
    On his sleep that is filled of me,
On his brow where the curved wisps clot and twine
    Carelessly,
On his lips where the light breaths come and go
    Unconsciously,
On his limbs in sleep at last laid low
    Helplessly,
I shall weep, oh, I shall weep, I know
    For joy or for misery.

D. H. LAWRENCE
Love Poems and Others, 1913

EPITHALAMIUM

HIGH in the organ-loft, with lilied hair,
 Love plied the pedals with his snowy foot,
 Pouring forth music like the scent of fruit,
And stirring all the incense-laden air;
We knelt before the altar's gold rail, where
 The priest stood robed, with chalice and palm-shoot,
 With music-men who bore citole and lute
Behind us, and the attendant virgins fair.
And so our red aurora flashed to gold,
 Our dawn to sudden sun; and all the while
The high-voiced children trebled clear and cold,
 The censer-boys went swinging down the aisle,
And far above, with fingers strong and sure,
Love closed our lives' triumphant overture.

SIR EDMUND GOSSE,
On Viol and Flute, 1873

WEDDING RINGS OF VARIOUS COUNTRIES AND PERIODS: PHOTOGRAPH BY EDWIN SMITH

THE BRIDESMAID: PAINTING BY JAMES TISSOT, *c.* 1882

THE BRIDESMAID

WHY am I dressed in these beautiful clothes?
   What is the matter with me?
I've been the bridesmaid for twenty-two brides;
   This time'll make twenty-three.
Twenty-two ladies I've helped off the shelf;
   No doubt it seems a bit strange:
Being the bridesmaid is no good to me;
   And I think I could do with a change.

Chorus

Why am I always the bridesmaid?
   Never the blushing bride?
      Ding-dong! wedding bells
      Only ring for other gels;
But some fine day –
   Oh, let it be soon! –
I shall wake up in the morning
   On my own honeymoon.

CHARLES COLLINS AND FRED W. LEIGH
Why am I always the Bridesmaid?, 1917
sung by LILY MORRIS

147

NEARNESS

Thy hand my hand,
Thine eyes my eyes,
All of thee
Caught and confused with me:
My hand thy hand,
My eyes thine eyes,
All of me
Sunken and discovered anew in thee.

No: still
A foreign mind,
A thought
By other yet uncaught;
A secret will
Strange as the wind:
The heart of thee
Bewildering with strange fire the heart in me.

Hand touches hand,
Eye to eye beckons,
But who shall guess
Another's loneliness?
Though hand grasp hand,
Though the eye quickens,
Still lone as night
Remain thy spirit and mine, past touch and sight.

JOHN FREEMAN
Memories of Childhood and Other Poems, 1919

FAITH

DEAR, if you change, I'll never choose again:
  Sweet, if you shrink, I'll never think of love;
Fair, if you fail, I'll judge all beauty vain;
  Wise, if too weak, more wits I'll never prove.
Dear, sweet, fair, wise, change, shrink, nor be not weak;
And, on my faith, my faith shall never break.

Earth with her flowers shall sooner heaven adorn;
  Heaven her bright stars through earth's dim globe shall move.
Fire, heat shall lose; and frosts of flames be born;
  Air, made to shine, as black as hell shall prove.
Earth, heaven, fire, air, the world transformed shall view,
Ere I prove false to faith, or strange to you.

ANONYMOUS
in *The First Book of Songs or Airs*
composed by John Dowland, 1597

THE OFFERING OF THE HEART

LIKE a drop of water is my heart
   Laid upon her soft and rosy palm,
Turned whichever way her hand doth turn,
   Trembling in an ecstasy of calm.

Like a broken rose-leaf is my heart,
   Held within her close and burning clasp,
Breathing only dying sweetness out,
   Withering beneath the fatal grasp.

Like a vapoury cloudlet is my heart,
   Growing into beauty near the sun,
Gaining rainbow hues in her embrace,
   Melting into tears when it is done.

Like mine own dear harp is this my heart,
   Dumb, without the hand that sweeps its strings;
Though the hand be careless or be cruel,
   When it comes, my heart breaks forth and sings.

SARAH WILLIAMS
'Youth and Maidenhood'
Twilight Hours, 1868

THE OFFERING OF THE HEART: FRENCH FIFTEENTH-CENTURY TAPESTRY

TWILIGHT: WATER-COLOUR BY PAUL KLEE, 1919

COME, COME, DEAR NIGHT!

COME, come, dear Night! Love's mart of kisses
    Sweet close of his ambitious line,
The fruitful summer of his blisses,
    Love's glory doth in darkness shine.

O come, soft rest of cares! come, Night!
    Come naked virtue's only tire,
The reapëd harvest of the light
    Bound up in sheaves of sacred fire.

       Love calls to war;
        Sighs his alarms,
      Lips his swords are,
       The field his arms.

Come, Night, and lay thy velvet hand
    On glorious Day's outfacing face;
And all thy crownëd flames command
    For torches to our nuptial grace.

       Love calls to war;
        Sighs his alarms,
      Lips his swords are,
       The field his arms . . .

GEORGE CHAPMAN
Hero and Leander, 1598

GOING TO BED

Come, Madam, come, all rest my powers defy;
Until I labour, I in labour lie.
The foe oft-times having the foe in sight,
Is tired with standing, though he never fight.
Off with that girdle, like heaven's zone glittering,
But a far fairer world encompassing.
Unpin that spangled breast-plate, which you wear
That th'eyes of busy fools may be stopped there.
Unlace yourself, for that harmonious chime
Tells me from you that now it is bed-time.
Off with that happy busk, which I envy,
That still can be, and still can stand so nigh.
Your gown, going off, such beauteous state reveals,
As when through flowery meads th'hill's shadow steals.
Off with that wiry coronet, and show
The hairy diadem which on you doth grow.
Now off with those shoes; and then softly tread
In this, love's hallow'd temple, this soft bed,
In such white robes heaven's angels used to be
Revealed to men; thou, angel, bring'st with thee
A heaven like Mahomet's paradise; and though
Ill spirits walk in white, we easily know
By this these angels from an evil sprite;
Those set our hairs, but these our flesh, upright.
　Licence my roving hands, and let them go
Before, behind, between, above, below.
Oh, my America, my new-found-land!
My kingdom, safest when with one man manned!

My mine of precious stones! My empery!
How blest am I in thus discovering thee!
To enter in these bonds is to be free;
Then, where my hand is set, my seal shall be.
    Full nakedness! All joys are due to thee;
As souls unbodied, bodies unclothed must be,
To taste whole joys. Gems which you women use
Are like Atlanta's ball cast in men's views;
That, when a fool's eye lighteth on a gem,
His earthly soul may covet that, not them.
Like pictures, or like books' gay coverings made
For laymen, are all women thus arrayed.
Themselves are only mystic books, which we
(Whom their imputed grace will dignify)
Must see revealed. Then, since that I may know,
As liberally as to thy midwife show
Thyself; cast all, yea, this white linen hence;
There is no penance due to innocence.
    To teach thee, I am naked first; why than,
What needst thou have more covering than a man?

JOHN DONNE, *Poems*, 1669
(written *c.* 1600)

THE ANGELS DANCE

Love bred on glances
'Twixt amorous eyes,
Like children's fancies,
Soon born, soon dies.
Gilt bitterness and smiling woe
Does oft bewitch poor lovers so,
As the false sense the unwary soul deceives
With baleful poison wrapped in lily leaves.

But hearts so chainëd
As goodness stands,
With truth unfeignëd
To couple hands:
Love being to all beauty blind,
Save the dear beauties of the mind.
Here Heaven is pleased, content, and all bliss shedding;
The angels are guests, and dance at this blest wedding.

ANONYMOUS (before 1656)
Bodley MS. *Mus. b.* 1

ANGEL DANCING: AUSTRIAN CARVING IN LIMEWOOD, EIGHTEENTH CENTURY

NUDE: PAINTING BY WALTER RICHARD SICKERT, *c.* 1908

ON HER GIRDLE

THAT which her slender waist confined
Shall now my joyful temples bind;
No monarch but would give his crown
His arms might do what this has done.

It was my heaven's extremest sphere,
The pale which held that lovely dear;
My joy, my grief, my hope, my love,
Did all within this circle move.

A narrow compass – and yet there
Dwelt all that's good, and all that's fair:
Give me but what this ribbon bound,
Take all the rest the sun goes round!

EDMUND WALLER, *Poems*, 1645

HER ARMS LIE OPEN

This hour be her sweet body all my song,
   Now the same heart-beat blends her gaze with mine,
   One parted fire, Love's silent countersign:
Her arms lie open, throbbing with their throng
Of confluent pulses, bare and fair and strong:
   And her deep-freighted lips expect me now,
   Amid the clustering hair that shrines her brow
Five kisses broad, her neck ten kisses long.

Lo, Love! thy heaven of Beauty; where a sun
   Thou shin'st; and art a white-winged moon to press
   By hidden paths to every hushed recess;
Yea, and with sinuous lightnings here anon
Of passionate change, an instant seen and gone,
   Shalt light the tumult of this loveliness.

DANTE GABRIEL ROSSETTI
in *The Ashley Library Catalogue*, IX, 1927
(written 1869)

HOUR OF FULFILMENT

IT is in the hour of the fulfilment of love between a man and a woman that the reckless affirmations of mutinous life may best be apprehended. It is then that the vain mind of man, confounded utterly by the roarings of desire, lies open at last to instruction from the senses, from those five unparagoned wits that have become in one snatched instant more piercingly sensible of God's true word than ever are the pelts of frogs to a touch from mortal fingers hot as fire. With lips pressed upon lips and with bodies of tragic flesh fast clinging, the Platonic ordinance is suddenly revoked, and spontaneously our separated halves spring back once more to their right predestined wholes. And what is contained in these supreme transports, as hollow of thought as they are deep charged with feeling? A single spirit of splendour, we hunt in triumph through forests of flame. We are the wind that bends the flower at the hour before day-break, the wave that shakes the firm rock, the forked lightning that cleaves the tree, down, down to the matrix of its roots. It is you that I am possessing. It is you to whom I give myself utterly, utterly. As two we met, but as one we are parted.

LLEWELYN POWYS, *Love and Death*, 1939

LAY YOUR SLEEPING HEAD, MY LOVE

Lay your sleeping head, my love,
Human on my faithless arm;
Time and fevers burn away
Individual beauty from
Thoughtful children, and the grave
Proves the child ephemeral:
But in my arms till break of day
Let the living creature lie,
Mortal, guilty, but to me
The entirely beautiful.

Soul and body have no bounds:
To lovers as they lie upon
Her tolerant enchanted slope
In their ordinary swoon,
Grave the vision Venus sends
Of supernatural sympathy,
Universal love and hope;
While an abstract insight wakes
Among the glaciers and the rocks
The hermit's sensual ecstasy.

Certainty, fidelity
On the stroke of midnight pass
Like vibrations of a bell,
And fashionable madmen raise
Their pedantic boring cry:
Every farthing of the cost,
All the dreaded cards foretell,
Shall be paid, but from this night
Not a whisper, not a thought,
Not a kiss nor look be lost.

Beauty, midnight, vision dies:
Let the winds of dawn that blow
Softly round your dreaming head
Such a day of sweetness show
Eye and knocking heart may bless,
Find the mortal world enough;
Noons of dryness see you fed
By the involuntary powers,
Nights of insult let you pass
Watched by every human love.

W. H. AUDEN, *Another Time*, 1940

HOTEL BEDROOM

TENDERNESS of evening sky: the light shrinking.
The mirror lifting a dulled eye to the plaster.
Breath of a city: multitude of delicate sounds
Off an unfamiliar horizon. The blind-cord stirring
Unevenly, like a pendant on the breast of twilight.

We have slept for some minutes, I discover: resuming now
In a room shades darker. And lie together, inert
In a kind of atonement, desire left to sleep on,
Almost like a bed-fellow, a third. And we,
In a moment of unsought grace, perfectly rhyming together,
A kind of plenary indulgence, are excused
All inquietude, all anxiety. And take pleasure
In the silhouette of the wardrobe: observing, too,
How the basin taps are marvellously defined
By twin faint stars. Myself, I ponder the world
Beyond these murmuring horizons, where nations await
No judgement, only sentence. And turn to picturing,
Quite small, as though at a great remove, and ringed
By nameless mountains that note the effect like mirrors,
The city of a blinding moment: the self-bright city
That will never again greet the mocked sun. Our world,
This moment, small and safe as a hired room,
And this nude room as rich to explore as the world.

The luggage waits to be opened on the stool.
The floor-boards speak discreetly in the corridor.
The cord moves, pendant in the rhythm of compassion.
We shall never lie here again. Already the room
Overlooks our one-night tenure. Vacantly exists
For tomorrow, always for tomorrow. Hears already
The rapid portering footsteps pause, and drop their burden.
Then the brisk engagement of the lock. Sees
Faces, not ours, that enter glancing around them
The same unspoken comment: 'Here, the exception.
This will never be home.' We are virtually gone already.
Might almost never have come. We moved too lightly
Through the public mind of this room – appeared too briefly
In the long exposure of the dark impersonal lens,
To be more, in that darkening eye, than ghosts.

Tenderness of the fugitive. Of the immaterial.
Of the soon-deleted. Of the fond once-in-a-while.
Of a blind-cord moving, softly, softly,
In time with the low breathing of maternal twilight.
Of rhyming together, once in an endless while.

LAURENCE WHISTLER, *The View from this Window*, 1956

165

AT VENUS' SHRINE

Soft, lovely, rose-like lips, conjoined with mine,
    Breathing out precious incense such,
Such as, at Paphos, smokes to Venus' shrine,
    Making my lips immortal with their touch,
My cheeks, with touch of thy soft cheeks divine,
    Thy soft warm cheeks which Venus favours much;
Those arms, such arms, which me embraced,
    Me with immortal cincture girding round,
    Of everlasting bliss, then bound
With her enfolded thighs in mine entangled,
And both in one self-soul placed,
    Made a hermaphrodite with pleasure ravished.
There heat for heat's, soul for soul's empire wrangled;
    Why died not I with love so largely lavished?
For waked (not finding truth of dreams before)
It secret vexeth ten times more.

BARNABE BARNES
Parthenophil and Parthenophe, 1593

S AMANTS HEUREUX: PAINTING BY JEAN-HONORÉ FRAGONARD, *c.* 1770

BACK-PLATE OF A CLOCK BY THOMAS CARTWRIGHT, EARLY EIGHTEENTH CENTURY

COUNTING THE BEATS

You, love, and I,
(He whispers) you and I,
And if no more than only you and I
What care you or I?

Counting the beats,
Counting the slow heart beats,
The bleeding to death of time in slow heart beats,
Wakeful they lie.

Cloudless day,
Night, and a cloudless day;
Yet the huge storm will burst upon their heads one day
From a bitter sky.

Where shall we be,
(She whispers) where shall we be,
When death strikes home, O where then shall we be
Who were you and I?

Not there but here,
(He whispers) only here,
As we are, here, together, now and here,
Always you and I.

Counting the beats,
Counting the slow heart beats,
The bleeding to death of time in slow heart beats,
Wakeful they lie.

ROBERT GRAVES, *Poems and Satires*, 1951

HE

Between her breasts is my home, between her breasts.
Three sides set on me space and fear, but the fourth side rests
Sure and a tower of strength, 'twixt the walls of her breasts.

Having known the world so long, I have never confessed
How it impresses me, how hard and compressed
Rocks seem, and earth, and air uneasy, and waters still ebbing west.

All things on the move, going their own little ways, and all
Jostling, people touching and talking and making small
Contacts and bouncing off again, bounce! bounce like a ball!

My flesh is weary with bounce and gone again! –
My ears are weary with words that bounce on them, and then
Bounce off again, meaning nothing. Assertions! Assertions! stones,
    women and men!

Between her breasts is my home, between her breasts.
Three sides set on me chaos and bounce, but the fourth side rests
Sure on a haven of peace, between the mounds of her breasts.

I am that I am, and no more than that: but so much
I am, nor will I be bounced out of it. So at last I touch
All that I am-not in softness, sweet softness, for she is such.

And the chaos that bounces and rattles like shrapnel, at least
Has for me a door into peace, warm dawn in the east
Where her bosom softens towards me, and the turmoil has ceased.

So I hope I shall spend eternity
With my face down buried between her breasts;
And my still heart full of security,
And my still hands full of her breasts.

D. H. LAWRENCE
'Song of a Man who is Loved'
Collected Poems, 1928

SHE

WAKING alone in a multitude of loves when morning's light
Surprised in the opening of her nightlong eyes
His golden yesterday asleep upon the iris
And this day's sun leapt up the sky out of her thighs
Was miraculous virginity old as loaves and fishes,
Though the moment of a miracle is unending lightning
And the shipyards of Galilee's footprints hide a navy of doves.

No longer will the vibrations of the sun desire on
Her deepsea pillow where once she married alone,
Her heart all ears and eyes, lips catching the avalanche
Of the golden ghost who ringed with his streams her mercury bone,
Who under the lids of her windows hoisted his golden luggage,
For a man sleeps where fire leapt down and she learns through his
    arm
That other sun, the jealous coursing of the unrivalled blood.

DYLAN THOMAS, 'On the Marriage of a Virgin'
Deaths and Entrances, 1946

WHILE SHE SLEEPS

WINDS, whisper gently whilst she sleeps,
  And fan her with your cooling wings;
Whilst she her drops of beauty weeps
  From pure and yet unrivalled springs.

Glide over beauty's field, her face,
  To kiss her lip and cheek be bold,
But with a calm and stealing pace,
  Neither too rude, nor yet too cold.

Play in her beams, and crisp her hair,
  With such a gale as wings soft love,
And with so sweet, so rich an air,
  As breathes from the Arabian grove.

A breath as hushed as lover's sigh,
  Or that unfolds the morning door;
Sweet as the winds that gently fly
  To sweep the Spring's enamelled floor.

Murmur soft music to her dreams,
  That pure and unpolluted run,
Like to the new-born crystal streams
  Under the bright enamoured sun.

But when she waking shall display
  Her light, retire within your bar:
Her breath is life, her eyes are day,
  And all mankind her creatures are.

CHARLES COTTON, *Poems*, 1689
(written *c.* 1660)

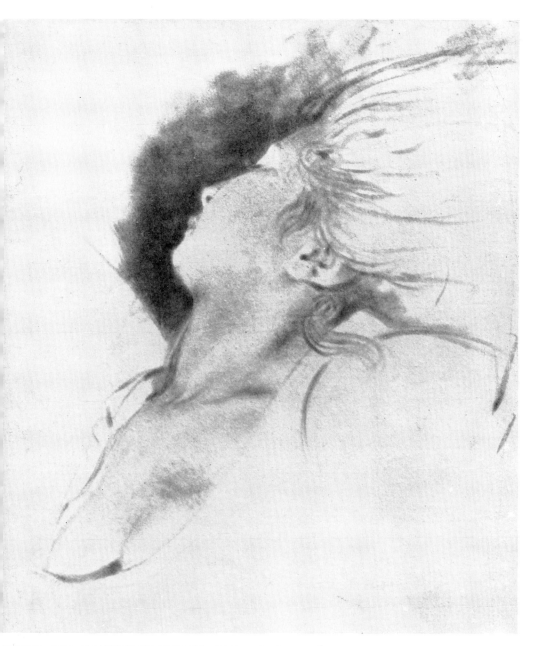

SLEEPING GIRL: DRAWING BY JOHN DOWNMAN, A.R.A., c. 1785

THE SKIES STOOP DOWN

. . . BEFORE he mounts the hill, I know
He cometh quickly: from below
Sweet gales, as from deep gardens, blow
Before him, striking on my brow.
　　In my dry brain my spirit soon,
　　Down-deepening from swoon to swoon,
　　Faints like a dazzled morning moon.

The wind sounds like a silver wire,
And from beyond the noon a fire
Is poured upon the hills, and nigher
The skies stoop down in their desire;
　　And, isled in sudden seas of light,
　　My heart, pierced thro' with fierce delight,
　　Bursts into blossom in his sight.

My whole soul waiting silently,
All naked in a sultry sky,
Droops blinded with his shining eye:
I *will* possess him or will die.
　　I will grow round him in his place,
　　Grow, live, die looking on his face,
　　Die, dying clasped in his embrace.

ALFRED, LORD TENNYSON
from 'Fatima', *Poems*, 1833

RADHA
GOING TO
MEET KRISHNA:
INDIAN MINIATURE
PAINTING
c. 1840

A YOUNG WIFE

THE pain of loving you
Is almost more than I can bear.
I walk in fear of you.
The darkness starts up where
You stand, and the night comes through
Your eyes when you look at me.
Ah never before did I see
The shadows that live in the sun!
Now every tall glad tree
Turns round its back to the sun
And looks down on the ground, to see
The shadow it used to shun.
At the foot of each glowing thing
A night lies looking up.
Oh, and I want to sing
And dance, but I can't lift up
My eyes from the shadows: dark
They lie spilt round the cup.

What is it? – Hark
The faint fine seethe in the air!
Like the seething sound in a shell!
It is death still seething where
The wild-flower shakes its bell
And the skylark twinkles blue –
The pain of loving you
Is almost more than I can bear.

D. H. LAWRENCE
Look, We have Come Through!, 1917

THE BEST YEARS WAIT

Do not expect again a phoenix hour,
The triple-towered sky, the dove complaining,
Sudden the rain of gold and heart's first ease
Tranced under trees by the eldritch light of sundown.

By a blazed trail our joy will be returning:
One burning hour throws light a thousand ways,
And hot blood stays into familiar gestures.
The best years wait, the body's plenitude.

Consider then, my lover, this is the end
Of the lark's ascending, the hawk's unearthly hover:
Spring season is over soon and first heatwave;
Grave-browed with cloud ponders the huge horizon.

Draw up the dew. Swell with pacific violence.
Take shape in silence. Grow as the clouds grew.
Beautiful brood the cornlands, and you are heavy;
Leafy the boughs – they also hide big fruit.

C. DAY LEWIS
From Feathers to Iron, 1931

THE LAST ROSE OF SUMMER

'Tis the last rose of summer
   Left blooming alone;
All her lovely companions
   Are faded and gone;
No flower of her kindred,
   No rose-bud is nigh,
To reflect back her blushes,
   Or give sigh for sigh . . .

THOMAS MOORE
Irish Melodies, 1821

A WOMAN
HOLDING
A FLOWER:
PAINTING BY
GWEN JOHN,
TWENTIETH
CENTURY

MOONLIGHT AFTER RAIN: PAINTING BY ATKINSON GRIMSHAW, 1883

AUTUMN

A MAN who has truly loved, though he may come to recognize the thousand incidental illusions into which love may have led him, will not recant its essential faith. He will keep his sense for the ideal and his power to worship. As a harp, made to vibrate to the fingers, gives some music to every wind, so the nature of man, necessarily susceptible to woman, becomes simultaneously sensitive to other influences, and capable of tenderness toward every object. A philosopher, a soldier, and a courtesan will express the same religion in different ways. In fortunate cases love may glide imperceptibly into settled domestic affections, giving them henceforth a touch of ideality; for when love dies in the odour of sanctity people venerate his relics. In other cases allegiance to the ideal may appear more sullenly, breaking out in whims, or in little sentimental practices which might seem half-conventional. Again, it may inspire a religious conversion, charitable works, or even artistic labours. Nature also is often a second mistress that consoles us for the loss of a first.

GEORGE SANTAYANA, *Little Essays*, 1920

MUSIC, when soft voices die,
Vibrates in the memory –
Odours, when sweet violets sicken,
Live within the sense they quicken ...

PERCY BYSSHE SHELLEY
Posthumous Poems, 1824

THE LEAF THAT FALLS

WHAT are we first? First, animals; and next,
    Intelligence at a leap; on whom
    Pale lies the distant shadow of the tomb,
And all that draweth on the tomb for text.
Into this state comes Love, the crowning sun:
    Beneath whose light the shadow loses form.
    We are the lords of life, and life is warm.
Intelligence and instinct now are one.
But Nature says: 'My children most they seem
    When they least know me: therefore I decree
    That they shall suffer.' Swift doth young Love flee,
And we stand waken'd, shivering from our dream.
Then if we study Nature we are wise.
    Thus do the few who live but with the day.
    The scientific animals are they. –
Lady, this is my sonnet to your eyes.

GEORGE MEREDITH, *Modern Love*, 1862

WHILE the blue noon above us arches
    And the poplar sheds disconsolate leaves,
    Tell me again why love bewitches
    And what love gives.

Is it the trembling finger that traces
    The eyebrow's curve, the curve of the cheek?
    The mouth that quivers, when the hand caresses
    But cannot speak?

No, not these, not in these is hidden
The secret, more than in other things:
Not only the touch of a hand can gladden
Till the blood sings.

It is the leaf that falls between us,
The bells that murmur, the shadows that move,
The autumnal sunlight that fades upon us:
These things are love.

It is the 'No, let us sit here longer,'
The 'Wait till tomorrow,' the 'Once I knew' –
These trifles, said as I touch your finger
And the clock strikes two.

The world is intricate, and we are nothing.
It is the complex world of grass,
The twig on the path, a look of loathing,
Feelings that pass –

These are the secret! And I could hate you
When, as I lean for another kiss,
I see in your eyes that I do not meet you,
And that love is this.

Rock meeting rock can know love better
Than eyes that stare or lips that touch.
All that we know in love is bitter,
And it is not much.

CONRAD AIKEN, 'Annihilation'
John Deth, and Other Poems, 1930

183

PICTURES IN AN ALBUM

I SEE you, a child
In a garden sheltered for buds and playtime,
Listening as if beguiled
By a fancy beyond your years and the flowering maytime.
The print is faded: soon there will be
No trace of that pose enthralling,
Nor visible echo of my voice distantly calling
'Wait! Wait for me!'

Then I turn the page
To a girl who stands like a questioning iris
By the waterside, at an age
That asks every mirror to tell what the heart's desire is.
The answer she finds in that oracle stream
Only time could affirm or disprove,
Yet I wish I was there to venture a warning, 'Love
Is not what you dream.'

Next you appear
As if garlands of wild felicity crowned you –
Courted, caressed, you wear
Like immortelles the lovers and friends around you.
'They will not last you, rain or shine,
They are but straws and shadows,'
I cry: 'Give not to those charming desperadoes
What was made to be mine.'

One picture is missing –
The last. It would show me a tree stripped bare
By intemperate gales, her amazing
Noonday of blossom spoilt which promised so fair.
Yet, scanning those scenes at your heyday taken,
I tremble, as one who must view
In the crystal a doom he could never deflect – yes, I too
Am fruitlessly shaken.

I close the book;
But the past slides out of its leaves to haunt me
And it seems, wherever I look,
Phantoms of irreclaimable happiness taunt me.
Then I see her, petalled in new-blown hours,
Beside me – 'All you love most there
Has blossomed again,' she murmurs, 'all that you missed there
Has grown to be yours.'

C. DAY LEWIS, *Word Over All*, 1943

SECOND WEDDING

'THEE, Mary, with this ring I wed,'
So, fourteen years ago, I said –
Behold another ring! – 'For what?'
'To wed thee o'er again – why not?'

With that first ring I married Youth,
Grace, Beauty, Innocence, and Truth;
Taste long admir'd, sense long rever'd,
And all my Molly then appear'd.
If she, by merit since disclos'd,
Prove twice the woman I suppos'd,
I plead that double merit now,
To justify a double vow.

Here then, today, (with faith as sure,
With ardour as intense, as pure,
As when, amidst the rites divine,
I took thy troth, and plighted mine),
To thee, sweet girl, my second ring
A token, and a pledge, I bring;
With this I wed, till death us part,
Thy riper virtues to my heart;
Those virtues, which, before untry'd,
The wife has added to the bride;
Those virtues, whose progressive claim
Endearing wedlock's very name,

My soul enjoys, my song approves,
For Conscience's sake, as well as Love's.
And why? – They show me every hour,
Honour's high thought, affection's power,
Discretion's deed, sound Judgment's sentence,
And teach me all things – but Repentance.

THE REV. SAMUEL BISHOP
Poetical Works, 1796

NOT theirs the vain, tumultuous bliss,
Whose only currency's a kiss,
Nor linkëd hands or meeting eyes,
But long-drawn mutual silences,
Community in trivial things,
The rare fantastic mood that brings
Wisdom and mirth unspeakable
Out of an insect or a shell.

E. H. W. MEYERSTEIN
In Merlin's Wood, 1922

PLEDGES AND MIRRORS

No man can tell but he that loves his children, how many delicious accents make a man's heart dance in the pretty conversation of those dear pledges: their childishness, their stammering, their little angers, their innocence, their imperfections, their necessities are so many little emanations of joy and comfort to him that delights in their persons and society; but he that loves not his wife and children, feeds a lioness at home, and broods a nest of sorrow.

JEREMY TAYLOR, *Twenty-five Sermons*, 1653

IN one soul we may be entertained and taken up with innumerable beauties. But in the soul of man there are innumerable infinities. One soul in the immensity of its intelligence is greater and more excellent than the whole world. The ocean is but the drop of a bucket to it, the heavens but a centre, the sun obscurity, and all ages but as one day; it being by its understanding a temple of eternity, and God's omnipresence, between which and the whole world there is no proportion. Its love is a dominion greater than that which Adam had in Paradise: and yet the fruition of it is but solitary. We need spectators, and other diversities of friends and lovers, in whose souls we might likewise dwell, and with whose beauties we might be crowned, and entertained: in all whom we can dwell exactly, and be present with them fully. Lest therefore the other depths and faculties of our souls should be desolate and idle they also are created to entertain us. And as in many mirrors we are so many other selves, so are we spiritually multiplied when we meet ourselves more sweetly, and live again, in other persons.

THOMAS TRAHERNE, *Centuries of Meditations*, 1908 (written *c.* 1670)

THE FAMILY: BRONZE BY HENRY MOORE, 1945

CONVERSATION PIECE: PAINTING, ENGLISH SCHOOL, *c.* 1745

REST

So, we'll go no more a-roving
  So late into the night,
Though the heart be still as loving,
  And the moon be still as bright.

For the sword outwears its sheath,
  And the soul wears out the breast,
And the heart must pause to breathe,
  And love itself have rest.

Though the night was made for loving,
  And the day returns too soon,
Yet we'll go no more a-roving
  By the light of the moon.

GEORGE GORDON, LORD BYRON
Poems, 1823

TO EARTHWARD

Love at the lips was touch
  As sweet as I could bear;
And once that seemed too much;
  I lived on air

That crossed me from sweet things
  The flow of – was it musk
From hidden grapevine springs
  Down hill at dusk?

I had the swirl and ache
  From sprays of honeysuckle
That when they're gathered shake
  Dew on the knuckle.

I craved strong sweets, but those
  Seemed strong when I was young;
The petal of the rose
  It was that stung.

Now no joy but lacks salt
  That is not dashed with pain
And weariness and fault;
  I crave the stain

Of tears, the aftermark
  Of almost too much love,
The sweet of bitter bark
  And burning clove.

When stiff and sore and scarred
  I take away my hand
From leaning on it hard
  In grass and sand,

The hurt is not enough:
  I long for weight and strength
To feel the earth as rough
  To all my length.

ROBERT FROST
New Hampshire, 1923

IN MY OWN FIELDS TO RIDE

... I LEAVE my neighbours to their thought;
  My choice it is, and pride,
On my own lands to find my sport,
  In my own fields to ride.

The hare herself no better loves
  The field where she was bred,
Than I the habit of these groves,
  My own inherited.

I know my quarries every one,
  The meuse where she sits low;
The road she chose today was run
  A hundred years ago.

The lags, the gills, the forest ways,
  The hedgerows one and all,
These are the kingdoms of my chase,
  And bounded by my wall;

Nor has the world a better thing,
  Though one should search it round,
Than thus to live one's own sole king
  Upon one's own sole ground ...

WILFRID SCAWEN BLUNT
  'The Old Squire',
  The Poetry of Wilfrid Blunt, 1898

GENTLEMAN WITH WHITE HORSE AND DOGS: PAINTING BY R. R. REINAGLE, R.A., 1816

CAPITAL OF A COLUMN, CHAPTER HOUSE, SOUTHWELL, *c.* 1300: PHOTOGRAPH BY EDWIN SMITH

THE CARVER IN STONE

. . . He carved in stone. Out of his quiet life
He watched as any faithful seaman charged
With tidings of the myriad-faring sea,
And thoughts and premonitions through his mind
Sailing as ships from strange and storied lands
His hungry spirit held, till all they were
Found living witness in the chiselled stone.
Slowly out of the dark confusion, spread
By life's innumerable venturings
Over his brain, he would triumph into the light
Of one clear mood, unblemished of the blind
Legions of errant thought that cried about
His rapt seclusion: as a pearl unsoiled,
Nay, rather washed to lonelier chastity,
In gritty mud. And then would come a bird,
A flower, or the wind moving upon a flower,
A beast at pasture, or a clustered fruit,
A peasant face as were the saints of old,
The leer of custom, or the bow of the moon
Swung in miraculous poise – some stray from the world
Of things created by the eternal mind
In joy articulate. And his perfect mood
Would dwell about the token of God's mood
Until in bird or flower or moving wind
Or flock or shepherd or the troops of heaven
It sprang in one fierce moment of desire
To visible form . . .

JOHN DRINKWATER
Swords and Ploughshares, 1915

A GLORY PAST AWAY

THERE was a time when meadow, grove, and stream,
    The earth, and every common sight,
        To me did seem
      Apparelled in celestial light,
The glory and the freshness of a dream.
It is not now as it hath been of yore; –
    Turn wheresoe'er I may,
      By night or day,
The things which I have seen I now can see no more.

    The rainbow comes and goes,
    And lovely is the rose;
    The moon doth with delight
Look round her when the heavens are bare;
    Waters on a starry night
      Are beautiful and fair;
The sunshine is a glorious birth;
But yet I know, where'er I go,
That there hath past away a glory from the earth . . .

WILLIAM WORDSWORTH
from 'Intimations of Immortality'
Poems, 1807

MIGHT-HAVE-BEEN

LOOK in my face; my name is Might-have been;
    I am also called No-more, Too-late, Farewell;
    Unto thine ear I hold the dead-sea shell
Cast up thy Life's foam-fretted feet between;
Unto thine eyes the glass where that is seen
    Which had life's form and Love's, but by my spell
    Is now a shaken shadow intolerable,
Of ultimate things unuttered the frail screen.

Mark me, how still I am! But should there dart
    One moment through thy soul the soft surprise
    Of that winged Peace which lulls the breath of sighs –
Then shalt thou see me smile, and turn apart
Thy visage to mine ambush at thy heart
    Sleepless with cold commemorative eyes.

DANTE GABRIEL ROSSETTI
'A Superscription', *Poems*, 1870

IMMORTAL LOVE

IMMORTAL Love, author of this great frame,
  Sprung from that beauty which can never fade,
How hath man parcelled out Thy glorious name,
  And thrown it on that dust which Thou hast made,
While mortal love doth all the title gain!
  Which, siding with invention, they together
Bear all the sway, possessing heart and brain
  (Thy workmanship) and give Thee share in neither.
Wit fancies beauty, beauty raiseth wit:
  The world is theirs; they two play out the game,
Thou standing by: and though Thy glorious name
  Wrought our deliverance from th' infernal pit,
Who sings Thy praise? Only a scarf or glove
Doth warm our hands, and make them write of love.

GEORGE HERBERT, *The Temple*, 1633

HANDS IN ADORATION: BRUSH DRAWING BY ALBRECHT DÜRER, 1508

MRS. OSWALD: PAINTING BY JOHN ZOFFANY, R.A., *c.* 1770

THE SETTING SUN

WHEN Phoebus glows with radiant gold
   In his meridian height,
What eye uninjured can behold
   Th'insufferable light?

But when, declining to the west,
   He shoots a feebler ray,
His charms in milder radiance dressed
   With pleasure we survey.

In height of bloom, thus Fulvia charmed,
   Thus tortured every heart;
Her dazzling eyes each breast alarmed,
   Each glance conveyed a dart.

Their lustre softened now by time,
   Less ardent is their fire:
Tho' amiable as in her prime –
   With safety we admire.

THE REV. RICHARD GRAVES
Euphrosyne, 1776

UNEASY CORRESPONDENT

I DON'T love you, not at all; on the contrary, I detest you—You're a naughty, gawky, foolish Cinderella. You never write to me; you don't love your husband; you know what pleasure your letters give him, and yet you haven't written him six lines, dashed off casually!

What do you do all day, Madam? What is the affair so important as to leave you no time to write to your devoted lover? What affection stifles and puts to one side the love, the tender and constant love you promised him? Of what sort can be that marvellous being, that new lover, who absorbs every moment, tyrannizes over your days, and prevents your giving any attention to your husband? Josephine, take care! One fine night the doors will be broken open, and there I'll be.

Indeed, I am very uneasy, my love, at receiving no news of you; write to me quickly, four pages, pages full of agreeable things which shall fill my heart with the pleasant feelings.

I hope before long to crush you in my arms and cover you with a million kisses burning as though beneath the equator.—BONAPARTE.

NAPOLEON BONAPARTE
Letter to the Empress Josephine, 13 November 1796

THE ARROW IN THE HEART

IF the clock strikes, the sound jars me; a million of hours will not bring back peace to my breast. The light startles me; the darkness terrifies me. I seem falling into a pit, without a hand to help me. She has deceived me, and the earth falls from under my feet; no object in nature is substantial, real, but false and hollow, like her faith on which I built my trust. She came (I knew not how) and sat by my side and was folded in my arms, a vision of love and joy, as if she had dropped from the Heavens to bless me by some especial dispensation of a favouring Providence, and make me amends for all; and now without any fault of mine but too much fondness, she has vanished from me, and I am left to perish. My heart is torn out of me, with every feeling for which I wished to live. The whole is like a dream, an effect of enchantment; it torments me, and it drives me mad. I lie down with it; I rise up with it; and see no chance of repose. I grasp at a shadow, I try to undo the past, and weep with rage and pity over my own weakness and misery. I spared her again and again (fool that I was) thinking what she allowed from me was love, friendship, sweetness, not wantonness. How could I doubt it, looking in her face, and hearing her words, like sighs breathed from the gentlest of all bosoms? I had hopes, I had prospects to come, the flattery of something like fame, a pleasure in writing, health even would have come back with her smile – she has blighted all, turned all to poison and childish tears. Yet the barbed arrow is in my heart – I can neither endure it, nor draw it out; for with it flows my life's blood.

WILLIAM HAZLITT, *Liber Amoris*, 1823

BY THE RIVER

I WAS tired
When we found the place,
The quiet place by the river,
Where the sun shines through the willows,
Dappling the dark water
With green and gold.

I thought:
This is the end, this is peace.
We will stay by the river;
We will listen to its soft music
And watch its deep flowing.
The whispering leaves will be silent,
The golden shadows will deepen,
The river will rise and caress us.
Gently it will rise and embrace us
And bear us away, together.

Joyfully
I turned to tell you these things.
But I was alone by the river.
A cold wind shivered the willows;
Slowly a leaf twisted down to the water
And was carried away.

ANNA MCMULLEN
in *New Britain*, 1933

ECHO

Come to me in the silence of the night;
  Come in the speaking silence of a dream;
Come with soft rounded cheeks and eyes as bright
  As sunlight on a stream;
    Come back in tears,
O memory, hope, love of finished years.

O dream how sweet, too sweet, too bitter sweet,
  Whose wakening should have been in Paradise,
Where souls brimful of love abide and meet;
  Where thirsting longing eyes
    Watch the slow door
That opening, letting in, lets out no more.

Yet come to me in dreams, that I may live
  My very life again though cold in death:
Come back to me in dreams, that I may give
  Pulse for pulse, breath for breath:
    Speak low, lean low,
As long ago, my love, how long ago!

CHRISTINA ROSSETTI
Goblin Market and Other Poems, 1862

ABSENCE

Dark house, by which once more I stand
   Here in the long unlovely street,
   Doors, where my heart was used to beat
So quickly, waiting for a hand,

A hand that can be clasped no more –
   Behold me, for I cannot sleep,
   And like a guilty thing I creep
At earliest morning to the door.

He is not here; but far away
   The noise of life begins again,
   And ghastly thro' the drizzling rain
On the bald street breaks the blank day.

ALFRED, LORD TENNYSON
In Memoriam, 1850

PRESENCE

EXPECTING Him, my door was open wide:
   Then I looked round
   If any lack of service might be found,
And saw Him at my side:
   How entered, by what secret stair,
   I know not, knowing only He was there.

T. E. BROWN
Old John, and Other Poems, 1893

THE BEST-BELOVED

E'EN like two little bank-dividing brooks,
　　That wash the pebbles with their wanton streams,
And having ranged and searched a thousand nooks,
　　Meet both at length in silver-breasted Thames,
　　　　Where in a greater current they conjoin:
So I my best-beloved's am; so he is mine.

E'en so we met; and after long pursuit,
　　E'en so we joined, we both became entire;
No need for either to renew a suit,
　　For I was flax, and he was flames of fire
　　　　Our firm-united souls did more than twine;
So I my best-beloved's am; so he is mine . . .

Nor time, nor place, nor chance, nor death can bow
　　My least desires unto the least remove;
He's firmly mine by oath; I his by vow;
　　He's mine by faith; and I am his by love;
　　　　He's mine by water; I am his by wine:
Thus I my best-beloved's am; thus he is mine.

He is my altar; I, his holy place;
　　I am his guest; and he, my living food;
I'm his by penitence; he mine by grace;
　　I'm his by purchase; he is mine by blood;
　　　　He's my supporting elm; and I his vine:
Thus I my best-beloved's am; thus he is mine . . .

FRANCIS QUARLES, *Emblems*, 1635

210

THE MAGDALEN: PAINTING BY ROGIER VAN DER WEYDEN, FIFTEENTH CENTURY

ABSTRACT PAINTING BY BEN NICHOLSON, AEGINA, 1957

ABSOLUTE BEAUTY

HE who has been instructed thus far in the science of Love, and has been led to see beautiful things in their due order and rank, when he comes toward the end of his discipline, will suddenly catch sight of a wondrous thing, beautiful with the absolute Beauty; – and this, Socrates, is the aim and end of all those earlier labours: – he will see a Beauty eternal, not growing or decaying, not waxing or waning; nor will it be fair here and foul there, nor depending on time or circumstance or place, as if fair to some, and foul to others: nor shall Beauty appear to him in the likeness of a face or hand, nor embodied in any sort of form whatever . . . whether of heaven or of earth; but Beauty absolute, separate, simple, and everlasting; which lending of its virtue to all beautiful things that we see born to decay, itself suffers neither increase nor diminution, nor any other change.

When a man proceeding onwards from terrestrial things by the right way of loving, once comes to sight of that Beauty, he is not far from his goal. And this is the right way wherein he should go or be guided in his love; he should begin by loving earthly things for the sake of the absolute loveliness, ascending to that as it were by degrees or steps, from the first to the second, and thence to all fair forms; and from fair forms to fair conduct, and from fair conduct to fair principles, until from fair principles he finally arrive at the ultimate principle of all, and learn what absolute Beauty is.

This life, my dear Socrates, said Diotima, if any life at all is worth living, is the life that a man should live, in the contemplation of absolute Beauty.

PLATO, *Symposium, c.* 370 B.C., translated by Robert Bridges in *The Spirit of Man,* 1916

THEN DAWNS THE INVISIBLE

. . . HE comes with western winds, with evening's wandering airs,
With that clear dusk of heaven that brings the thickest stars.
Winds take a pensive tone, and stars a tender fire,
And visions rise, and change, which kill me with desire –

Desire for nothing known in my maturer years,
When Joy grew mad with awe at counting future tears.
When, if my spirit's sky was full of flashes warm,
I knew not whence they came, from sun or thunderstorm.

But first a hush of peace – a soundless calm descends;
The struggle of distress and fierce impatience ends;
Mute music soothes my breast – unuttered harmony,
That I could never dream till Earth was lost to me.

Then dawns the Invisible; the Unseen its truth reveals;
My outward sense is gone, my inward essence feels:
Its wings are almost free – its home, its harbour found,
Measuring the gulf, it stoops – and dares the final bound.

Oh! dreadful is the check – intense the agony –
When the ear begins to hear, and the eye begins to see;
When the pulse begins to throb, the brain to think again;
The soul to feel the flesh, and the flesh to feel the chain!

Yet I would lose no sting, would wish no torture less;
The more that anguish racks, the earlier it will bless;
And robed in fires of hell, or bright with heavenly shine,
If it but herald death, the vision is divine! . . .

EMILY BRONTË, from 'Silent is the house'
Complete Poems, 1941 (written in 1845)

GOD

But what do I love when I love Thee? Not beauty of bodies, nor the fair harmony of time, nor the brightness of the light, so gladsome to our eyes, nor sweet melodies of varied songs, nor the fragrant smell of flowers, and ointments, and spices, not manna and honey, not limbs acceptable to embracements of flesh. None of these I love, when I love my God; and yet I love a kind of light, and melody, and fragrance, and meat, and embracement, when I love my God, the light, melody, fragrance, meat, embracement of my inner man: where there shineth unto my soul, what space cannot contain, and there soundeth, what time beareth not away, and there smelleth, what breathing disperseth not, and there tasteth, what eating diminisheth not, and there clingeth, what satiety divorceth not. This is what I love, when I love my God.

SAINT AUGUSTINE, *Confessions*, written A.D. 400
translated by E. B. Pusey

We apprehend Him in the alternate voids and fulnesses of a cathedral; in the space that separates the salient features of a picture; in the living geometry of a flower, a seashell, an animal; in the pauses and intervals between the notes of music, in their difference and sonority; and, finally, on the plane of conduct, in the love and gentleness, the confidence and humility, which give beauty to the relationships between human beings.

ALDOUS HUXLEY

215

A QUICKNESS

FALSE life! a foil, and no more, when
    Wilt thou be gone?
Thou foul deception of all men,
That would not have the true come on!

Thou art a moon-like toil; a blind
    Self-posing state;
A dark contest of waves and wind;
A mere tempestuous debate.

Life is a fixed, discerning light,
    A knowing joy;
No chance, or fit: but ever bright
And calm and full, yet doth not cloy.

'Tis such a blissful thing, that still
    Doth vivify,
And shine and smile, and hath the skill
To please without eternity.

Thou art a toilsome mole, or less
    A moving mist.
But life is, what none can express,
A quickness, which my God hath kissed.

HENRY VAUGHAN
Silex Scintillans, 1655

PORTRAIT
OF A MAN:
PAINTING BY
DIRK BOUTS,
1462

FROST ON A WINDOW PANE: PHOTOGRAPH BY CLARENCE PONTING

WINTER

I, SINGULARLY moved
To love the lovely that are not beloved,
Of all the seasons, most
Love Winter, and to trace
The sense of the Trophonian pallor on her face.
It is not death, but plenitude of peace;
And the dim cloud that does the world enfold
Hath less the characters of dark and cold
Than warmth and light asleep,
And correspondent breathing seems to keep
With the infant harvest, breathing soft below
Its eider coverlet of snow . . .

COVENTRY PATMORE
The Unknown Eros, 1878

How simple is my burden every day
　Now you have died, till I am also dead,
The words 'Forgive me', that I could not say,
　The words 'I am sorry', that you might have said.

FRANCES CORNFORD, *Collected Poems*, 1954

219

IN TIME

In time the strong and stately turrets fall,
  In time the rose and silver lilies die,
In time the monarchs captives are, and thrall,
  In time the sea and rivers are made dry;
The hardest flint in time doth melt asunder;
  Still living fame in time doth fade away;
The mountains proud we see in time come under;
  And earth, for age, we see in time decay.
The sun in time forgets for to retire
  From out the east where he was wont to rise;
The basest thoughts we see in time aspire,
  And greedy minds in time do wealth despise.
Thus all, sweet Fair, in time must have an end,
Except thy beauty, virtues, and thy friend.

GILES FLETCHER, *Licia*, 1593

TO AGE

WELCOME, old friend! These many years
   Have we lived door by door:
The Fates have laid aside their shears
   Perhaps for some few more.

I was indocile at an age
   When better boys were taught,
But thou at length hath made me sage,
   If I am sage in aught.

Little I know from other men,
   Too little they from me,
But thou hast pointed well the pen
   That writes these lines to thee.

Thanks for expelling Fear and Hope,
   One vile, the other vain;
One's scourge, the other's telescope,
   I shall not see again:

Rather what lies before my feet
   My notice shall engage –
He who hath braved Youth's dizzy heat
   Dreads not the frost of Age.

WALTER SAVAGE LANDOR
in *The Examiner*, 1852

THIS FRAGILE FRAME

ONCE I was part of the music I heard
  On the boughs or sweet between earth and sky,
  For joy of the beating of wings on high
My heart shot into the breast of the bird.

I hear it now and I see it fly,
  And a life in wrinkles again is stirred;
  My heart shoots into the breast of the bird
As it will for sheer love till the last long sigh.

GEORGE MEREDITH, *Poems*, 1912

I LOOK into my glass,
  And view my wasting skin,
And say 'Would God it came to pass
  My heart had shrunk as thin!'

For then, I, undistrest
  By hearts grown cold to me,
Could lonely wait my endless rest
  With equanimity.

But Time, to make me grieve,
  Part steals, lets part abide;
And shakes this fragile frame at eve
  With throbbings of noontide.

THOMAS HARDY, *Wessex Poems
and Other Verses*, 1898

AN OLD PEASANT WOMAN: PAINTING BY EDGAR DEGAS, 1857

A MAN AND HIS WIFE: STAFFORDSHIRE POTTERY GROUP, *c.* 1840

MY OLD DUTCH

We've been together now for forty years,
An' it don't seem a day too much;
There ain't a lady livin' in the land
As I'd swop for my dear old Dutch.

    I calls 'er Sal;
'Er proper name is Sairer;
An' yer may find a gal
As you'd consider fairer.
She ain't a angel – she can start
A-jawin' till it makes yer smart;
She's just a *woman*, bless 'er 'eart,
    Is my old gal . . .

We've been together now for forty years,
An' it don't seem a day too much;
There ain't a lady livin' in the land
As I'd swop for my dear old Dutch.

    I sees yer, Sal –
Yer pretty ribbons sportin':
Many years now, old gal,
Since them young days of courtin'.
I ain't a coward, still I trust
When we've to part, as part we must,
That Death may come and take me fust
    To wait . . . my pal.

ALBERT CHEVALIER, *My Old Dutch*, 1892

HOUSE OF REST

Now all the world she knew is dead
  In this small room she lives her days,
The wash-hand stand and single bed
  Screened from the public gaze.

The horse-brass shines, the kettle sings,
  The cup of China tea
Is tasted among cared-for things
  Ranged round for me to see –

Lincoln, by Valentine and Co.,
  Now yellowish brown and stained,
But there some fifty years ago
  Her Harry was ordained;

Outside the Church at Woodhall Spa
  The smiling groom and bride,
And here's his old tobacco jar
  Dried lavender inside.

I do not like to ask if he
  Was 'High' or 'Low' or 'Broad'
Lest such a question seem to be
  A mockery of Our Lord.

Her full grey eyes look far beyond
  The little room and me
To village church and village pond
  And ample rectory.

She sees her children each in place
   Eyes downcast as they wait,
She hears her Harry murmur Grace,
   Then heaps the porridge plate.

Aroused at seven, to bed by ten,
   They fully lived each day,
Dead sons, so motor-bike-mad then,
   And daughters far away.

Now when the bells for Eucharist
   Sound in the Market Square,
With sunshine struggling through the mist
   And Sunday in the air,

The veil between her and her dead
   Dissolves and shows them clear,
The Consecration Prayer is said
   And all of them are near.

JOHN BETJEMAN
A Few Late Chrysanthemums, 1954

AND STILL TO LOVE

... THY needles, once a shining store,
For my sake restless heretofore,
Now rust disused, and shine no more,
     My Mary! ...

Thy silver locks, once auburn bright,
Are still more lovely in my sight
Than golden beams of orient light,
     My Mary!

For, could I view nor them nor thee,
What sight worth seeing could I see?
The sun would rise in vain for me,
     My Mary!

Partakers of thy sad decline,
Thy hands their little force resign;
Yet, gently prest, press gently mine,
     My Mary!

And then I feel that still I hold
A richer store ten thousandfold
Than misers fancy in their gold,
     My Mary! ...

And still to love, though prest with ill,
In wintry age to feel no chill,
With me is to be lovely still,
     My Mary! ...

WILLIAM COWPER
Life and Letters, 1803 (written 1793)

THEN FAREWELL, WORLD!

LEAVE me, O Love, which reachest but to dust,
  And thou, my mind, aspire to higher things.
Grow rich in that which never taketh rust:
  Whatever fades, but fading pleasure brings.
Draw in thy beams, and humble all thy might
  To that sweet yoke where lasting freedoms be,
Which breaks the clouds and opens forth the light
  That doth both shine and give us sight to see.
O, take fast hold! Let that light be thy guide
  In this small course which birth draws out to death,
And think how evil becometh him to slide
  Who seeketh heaven, and comes of heavenly breath.
Then farewell, world! thy uttermost I see:
Eternal Love, maintain thy life in me!

SIR PHILIP SIDNEY, in *Arcadia*, 1598

PURE DEATH

WE looked, we loved, and therewith instantly
Death became terrible to you and me.
By love we disenthralled our natural terror
From every comfortable philosopher
Or tall, grey doctor of divinity:
Death stood at last in his true rank and order.

It happened soon, so wild of heart were we,
Exchange of gifts grew to a malady:
Their worth rose always higher on each side
Till there seemed nothing but ungivable pride
That yet remained ungiven, and this degree
Called a conclusion not to be denied.

Then we at least bethought ourselves, made shift
And simultaneously this final gift
Gave: each with shaking hand unlocks
The sinister, long, brass-bound coffin-box,
Unwraps pure death, with such bewilderment
As greeted our love's first acknowledgement.

ROBERT GRAVES, *Poems*, 1927
(revised later)

PRAYER TO MY LORD

IF ever Thou didst love me, love me now,
   When round me beat the flattering vans of life,
Kissing with rapid breath my lifted brow.
   Love me, if ever, when the murmuring of strife
In each dark byway of my being creeps,
   When pity and pride, passion and passion's loss
   Wash wavelike round the world's eternal Cross.
Till 'mid my fears a new-born love indignant leaps.

If ever Thou canst love me, love me yet,
   When sweet, impetuous loves within me stir
And the frail portals of my spirit fret –
   The love of love, that makes Heaven heavenlier,
The love of earth, of birds, children and light,
   Love of this bitter, lovely native land . . .
   O, love me when sick with all these I stand
And Death's far-rumoured wings beat on the lonely night.

JOHN FREEMAN, Fifty Poems, 1916

AND DEATH SHALL HAVE NO DOMINION

AND death shall have no dominion.
Dead men naked they shall be one
With the man in the wind and the west moon;
When their bones are picked clean and the clean bones gone,
They shall have stars at elbow and foot;
Though they go mad they shall be sane,
Though they sink through the sea they shall rise again;
Though lovers be lost love shall not;
And death shall have no dominion.

And death shall have no dominion.
Under the windings of the sea
They lying long shall not die windily;
Twisting on racks when sinews give way,
Strapped to a wheel, yet they shall not break;
Faith in their hands shall snap in two,
And the unicorn evils run them through;
Split all ends up they shan't crack;
And death shall have no dominion.

And death shall have no dominion.
No more may gulls cry at their ears
Or waves break loud on the seashores;
Where blew a flower may a flower no more
Lift its head to the blows of the rain;
Though they be mad and dead as nails,
Heads of the characters hammer through daisies;
Break in the sun till the sun breaks down,
And death shall have no dominion.

DYLAN THOMAS, *Twenty-five Poems*, 1936

THE BURIAL OF COUNT ORGAZ: DETAIL OF PAINTING BY EL GRECO, 1586

MONUMENT TO SIR WILLIAM DYER, COLMWORTH, BEDFORDSHIRE, 1641

THIS QUIET DUST

My dearest dust, could not thy hasty day
Afford thy drowszy patience leave to stay
One hower longer: so that we might either
Sate up, or gone to bedd together?
But since thy finisht labor hath possest
Thy weary limbs with early rest,
Enjoy it sweetly: and thy widdowe bride
Shall soone repose her by thy slumbring side.
Whose business, now, is only to prepare
My nightly dress, and call to prayre:
Mine eyes wax heavy and ye day growes old.
The dew falls thick, my belovd growes cold.
Draw, draw ye closed curtaynes: and make roome:
My deare, my dearest dust; I come, I come.

> LADY CATHERINE DYER
> Epitaph on the monument to
> Sir William Dyer at Colmworth, 1641
> (illustrated on the opposite page)

THIS quiet dust was gentlemen and ladies,
    And lads and girls;
Was laughter and ability and sighing,
    And frocks and curls.
This passive place a summer's nimble mansion,
    Where bloom and bees
Fulfill'd their oriental circuit,
    Then ceased, like these.

> EMILY DICKINSON, *The Single Hound*, 1914

HOLY THORN

... Now snow softly falls, and weaves
A silver dream of summer eves,
And the tree stretches twig and bough,
Thinking the glimmering weight of snow
Honey-hearted as blossom was
That once leaned over the tall, May grass.
The sap remembers how, between
Night and morning, a wind serene
Brushed the ghost petals, and set moving
Love, and the fragrances of loving;
And the tree muses how night's blue
Trembled to green, and how strange dew,
Repeating heaven star for star,
Made the field unfamiliar.

And now, like that lost nightingale
Who sang till the moon burned cold and pale
On the grave pyre of dawn, the air
Is tuned to an invisible, rare
Music; and luminous-feathered song
Dives and wheels and flits among
The listening branches, till the tree,
Lit with antiphonal ecstasy
Jets from the sealed and silent ground
In crystal fountains, whose clear sound
Sings upward to the singing sky
A rapt and fiery symphony.
And while the tree resolves all pain
In the pure silver of that strain,

Behold, in darkness suddenly
Another and a holier tree
Invests with candid, radiant light
The long, dusk-haunted groves of night;
Those blossoms gleam more milky-fair
Than Eve's blanched flowers in Eden were;
Those boughs spread out like arms to take
A word to shelter, for love's sake,
And at its heart those green leaves fold
A child, whose head is ringed with gold.
Is he a king? his courtiers then
Are falcons and throstle, dove and wren;
A general? his armies are
Butterflies winging the wide air;
A god? his only priestess is
Maid Mary kneeling in the grass . . .
Now through her tears the petals fall
Red and white and beautiful,
Until she prays in snow, and stark
A thorn-crowned tree upbraids the dark
A moment, and the vision
Melts in the morning, and is gone.
The bells ring out for Christmas day
With 'Gloria' and 'Gloria'
And on the eastern horizon
Flowers a rose-enfolding sun,
Fulfilling life . . .

VIOLA GARVIN, in *An Anthology of Christmas Prose and Verse*, 1928

BEFORE DAWN

. . . Bull unto bull with hollow throat
Makes echo every hill,
Cold sheep in pastures thick with snow
The air with bleatings fill;
While of his mother's heart this Babe
  Takes His sweet will.

All flowers and butterflies lie hid,
The blackbird and the thrush
Pipe but a little as they flit
Restless from bush to bush;
Even to the robin Gabriel hath
  Cried softly, 'Hush!'

Now night's astir with burning stars
In darkness of the snow;
Burdened with frankincense and myrrh
And gold the Strangers go
Into a dusk where one dim lamp
  Burns faintly, Lo!

No snowdrop yet its small head nods,
In winds of winter drear;
No lark at casement in the sky
Sings matins shrill and clear;
Yet in this frozen mirk the Dawn
  Breathes, Spring is here!

WALTER DE LA MARE
The Veil, and Other Poems, 1921

MADONNA AND CHILD: SIXTEENTH-CENTURY FLORENTINE TERRACOTTA RELIEF

THE SNOWDROP: MEZZOTINT FROM 'THE TEMPLE OF FLORA', 1807

THE YEAR IS DEAD

ORPHAN hours, the year is dead;
  Come and sigh, come and weep;
Merry hours, smile instead,
  For the year is but asleep:
See, it smiles as it is sleeping,
Mocking your untimely weeping.

As an earthquake rocks a corse
  In its coffin in the clay,
So white winter, that rough nurse,
  Rocks the dead-cold year today.
Solemn hours! wail aloud
For your mother in her shroud.

As the wild air stirs and sways
  The tree-swung cradle of a child,
So the breath of these rude days
  Rocks the year: – be calm and mild,
Trembling hours; she will arise
With new love within her eyes . . .

PERCY BYSSHE SHELLEY
Posthumous Poems, 1824

NOTES ON THE ILLUSTRATIONS
The names of the owners of works illustrated are printed in italics

Frontispiece. SIR PETER PAUL RUBENS (1577–1640). The painter and his first wife, Isabella Brandt. *c.* 1609. Oil on canvas. 70½ × 53½ in. *Munich, Altere Pinakothek.*

19. PABLO PICASSO (*b.* 1881). Mother and child. 1905. Gouache. 25¼ × 19⅞ in. *Private Collection.* (Copyright S.P.A.D.E.M. Paris.)

20. ALBRECHT DÜRER (1471–1528). Young hare. 1502. Water-colour and body colour. 9⅞ × 8⅞ in. *Vienna, Albertina Collection.*

25. MARBLE MONUMENT to Ann Moore, a child. 1683. *Church of St. John the Baptist, Plumpton, Northamptonshire.*

26. CAESAR VAN EVERDINGEN (1606–79). A child with an apple and a bird. 1664. Oil on canvas. 39½ × 33 in. *National Loan Collection Trust.*

35. JEAN-BAPTISTE-SIMÉON CHARDIN (1699–1779). La toilette du matin. 1741. Oil on canvas. 19¼ × 15 in. *Stockholm, National Museum.*

36. ISAAC TAYLOR (1759–1829). Ann and Jane Taylor. 1791. Oil on canvas. 17¾ × 13½ in. *London, National Portrait Gallery.*

Ann Taylor (1782–1866) and her sister Jane (1783–1824) wrote *Rhymes for the Nursery*, 1806, and other verses for children including 'Twinkle, twinkle, little star'. This portrait by their father shows the sisters in their garden at Lavenham in Suffolk.

41. FRANÇOIS BOUCHER (1703–70). Head of a boy. Black, red and white chalks, on grey paper. 8½ × 7¼ in. *London, British Museum.*

42. PAUL GAUGUIN (1848–1903). Jeune baigneurs Bretons. 1888. Oil on canvas. 36⅛ × 28½ in. *London, O'Hana Galleries.*

47. SUZANNE EISENDIECK. Le chapeau aux roses. *c.* 1930. Oil on canvas. 25 × 19 in. *London, Leger Gallery.*

48. ARTIST UNKNOWN, DUTCH SCHOOL. Maurice, Count of Nassau (1567–1625), at the age of fourteen. 1580. Oil on panel. 40¾ × 28⅝ in. *The Hague, Kon. Huisarchief.* By gracious permission of H.M. the Queen of the Netherlands.

57. VALENTINE. *c.* 1840. *London, Victoria and Albert Museum.* (The Post Office Notice reproduced on page 56 comes from the same source.)

58. MARGARET SARAH CARPENTER (1793–1872). The love letter. *c.* 1840. Water-colour. 13 × 10 in. *London: Messrs. Frost & Reed.*

Mrs. Carpenter was a portrait painter who frequently exhibited at the Royal Academy. Her *genre* pictures, such as this, have almost a Pre-Raphaelite quality and technique.

63. NEEDLEWORK PICTURE. Shepherd and shepherdess. English, early eighteenth century. Tent stitch. 21 × 17 in. *London, Messrs. Arditti & Mayorcas.*

64. CHELSEA PORCELAIN GROUP. Lovers. *c.* 1750. Crown and trident mark, in blue. 8½ in. high. Photograph by Jack Skeel. *London, British Museum.*

69. WATCH AND CHATELAINE. Signed 'Julien le Roy'. French, eighteenth century. Gold, set with topaz and diamonds in silver collets. Photograph by Edwin Smith. *London, Victoria and Albert Museum.*

70. JAN VERMEER OF DELFT (1632–75). The lacemaker. *c.* 1665. Oil on canvas. 9½ × 8¼ in. *Paris, Musée du Louvre.*

79. PIERRE AUGUSTE RENOIR (1841–1919). Baigneuse. *c.* 1890. Oil on canvas. 15 × 11½ in. *Sir Chester Beatty: Collection of Edith Beatty.* (Copyright S.P.A.D.E.M. Paris.)

80. FRANÇOIS AUGUSTE RODIN (1840–1917). Le Printemps. 1884. Plaster. 25⅝ in. high. *Paris, Musée Rodin.* (Copyright S.P.A.D.E.M. Paris.)

85. STAINED GLASS WINDOW. Adam and Eve in the Garden of Eden. German, early sixteenth century. 20 × 13 in. *London, Victoria and Albert Museum.*

86. HENRY TONKS (1862–1937). The orchard. Oil on canvas. 26 × 18 in. *City of Birmingham Art Gallery.*

Tonks was a Fellow of the Royal College of Surgeons before he abandoned his medical career and took up painting. He became Slade Professor of Fine Art at University College.

91. THOMAS GAINSBOROUGH (1727–88). Haymaker and sleeping girl. *c.* 1786. Oil on canvas. 88 × 57 in. *Boston, Museum of Fine Arts.*

This unfinished picture, which has only become generally known since its acquisition by the Boston Museum in 1953, is, as Professor Waterhouse writes, 'painted with a greater breadth and boldness of handling than Gainsborough ever showed before . . . in a style which looks backwards to Rubens and forward to Renoir'. It dates from Gainsborough's last years.

92. SÈVRES PORCELAIN GROUP. Le baiser donné. Modelled by Falconet, 1765. 7 in. high. Photograph by Jack Skeel. *London, British Museum.*

101. COLOURED WAX. A gardener. Second quarter of the nineteenth century. Signed 'Lewi'. 7½ in. diameter. *London, Victoria and Albert Museum.*

102. NICHOLAS VAN VERENDAEL (1640–91). Flower piece. Oil on panel. 12½ × 9½ in. Exhibited at the Slatter Gallery, London, 1957. *Mrs. D. C. Douglas Robertson.*

107. PREHISTORIC ROCK PAINTING. Dancers. Neolithic Age, *c.* 10,000 B.C. Oued Mertoutek gorge, Hoggar Mountains, Sahara. Reproduction by courtesy of the Musée de l'Homme, Paris.

108. MEISSEN PORCELAIN GROUP. Dancers. Modelled by J. F. Eberlein, *c.* 1735. 5½ in. high. Photograph by F. Jewell-Harrison. *Bedford, The Cecil Higgins Museum.*

This Meissen group was copied or adapted subsequently at Chelsea and Bow, but the delicacy of the original was never equalled.

113. ADÈLE ANAÏS TOUDOUZE (1822–99). Ballroom gowns. Fashion plate from *Le Follet*, 1853. Hand-coloured engraving. 7¾ × 5½ in. *London, Victoria and Albert Museum.*

An example from what Mr. Vyvyan Holland, the authority on this subject, calls 'the Golden Age of the fashion-plate', when the illustrations in the French magazines of *les modes* were not only exquisite works of the engraver's and colourist's art, but also took on some of the form of the conversation piece.

114. 'DANCE, LITTLE LADY.' Lauri Devine dancing in Charles B. Cochran's original production of Noël Coward's revue at the London Pavilion, *This Year of Grace*, 1928. The masks were designed by Oliver Messel. Photograph by Lenare from the Mander and Mitchenson Collection.

123. STAFFORDSHIRE SALTGLAZE POTTERY GROUP. *c.* 1730. 6¼ in. high. Photograph by Edwin Smith. *London, British Museum.*

A fine specimen of the very rare 'pew groups', notable for their droll humour and 'primitive' modelling, which preceded the more familiar Staffordshire figures of the late eighteenth century.

124. NICOLAS MAES (1632–93). Card players. Oil on canvas. 48 × 40 in. *London, National Gallery.*

An early work by Maes, who was a pupil of Rembrandt in 1650, and later worked in Antwerp.

129. JEAN ANTOINE WATTEAU (1684–1721). A man playing a hurdy-gurdy or *vielle*. Oil on canvas. 8⅝ × 6¾ in. *Birmingham, The Barber Institute of Fine Arts.*

Probably a very late work by Watteau, and considered by some to be a self-portrait. The reproduction here is very little smaller than the original.

130. SIR PETER LELY (1618–80). A lady of the Lake family. Detail from conversation piece of two ladies. *c.* 1660. Oil on canvas. 50 × 73 in. *London, Tate Gallery.*

135. GABRIEL METSU (1630–67). The letter reader. Oil on panel. 20½ × 16 in. *Sir Alfred Beit, Bart.*

Sir Alfred Beit also owns a companion picture, 'The letter writer', showing a young man writing the letter which the lady is reading here.

136. ENGRAVED SILVER TAZZA. London, 1688. Probably made by William Gamble. 9¼ in. diameter. *New Jersey, Montclair Art Museum.*

145. WEDDING RINGS. Photograph by Edwin Smith. *London, Cameo Corner.*

Most of the rings illustrated are English, of the Victorian period, but the two at the top right-hand corner are modern Nigerian rings, the thin ring in the centre of the lower group is Georgian, and the ring to the left of that is Indian.

146. JAMES JOSEPH JACQUES TISSOT (1836–1902). The brides-maid. *c.* 1882. Oil on canvas. 58 × 40 in. *Leeds, City Art Gallery.*

151. FRENCH TAPESTRY. The offering of the heart. Probably Arras work, early fifteenth century. Woven in wool and silk. 8 ft. 6 in. × 8 ft. 10 in. *Paris, Musée du Louvre.*

152. PAUL KLEE (1879–1940). Twilight. 1919. Water-colour. $8\frac{1}{4} \times$ $5\frac{1}{4}$ in. *London, Messrs. Roland, Browse & Delbanco.*

157. CARVING IN LIMEWOOD, GILT. An angel. Austrian, mid-eighteenth century. 57 in. high. *London, Victoria and Albert Museum.*

158. WALTER RICHARD SICKERT (1860–1942). Nude, Mornington Crescent. *c.* 1908. Oil on canvas. 20 × 18 in. *London, Messrs. Roland, Browse & Delbanco.*

167. JEAN-HONORÉ FRAGONARD (1732–1806). Les amants heureux. *c.* 1770. Oil on canvas. $19\frac{3}{4} \times 24$ in. *Private Collection.*

168. BACK-PLATE OF A CLOCK, by the Royal clock-maker, Thomas Cartwright (apprenticed 1693, died 1741). Photograph by courtesy of Messrs. Phillips of Hitchin Ltd. *London: R. I. H. Paul, Esq.*

173. JOHN DOWNMAN, A.R.A. (1750–1824). A sleeping girl. *c.* 1785. Black chalk and stump. $10\frac{3}{4} \times 9\frac{1}{2}$ in. In the Paul Oppé Collection. *Miss Armide Oppé and Mr. Denys Oppé.*

174. INDIAN MINIATURE. Radha going to meet Krishna by night. Guler (Punjab hills). *c.* 1840. $11\frac{1}{4} \times 8\frac{1}{4}$ in. *London, Victoria and Albert Museum.*

In this picture of the legendary Radha stealing out by night to meet her lover Krishna – seen in the top left-hand corner – the vignettes at the foot symbolize various aspects of love fulfilled or frustrated.

179. GWEN JOHN (1876–1939). A woman holding a flower. Oil on canvas. 12¾ × 10½ in. *City of Birmingham Art Gallery.*

180. ATKINSON GRIMSHAW (1836–93). Moonlight after rain. 1883. Oil on canvas. 17½ × 13½ in. *London, Mrs. Robert Frank.*

A Leeds man, Atkinson Grimshaw painted the poetry of night – of lamp-lit streets and rain-washed pavements. Perhaps something of a pre-Raphaelite in technique, he imbued all his paintings, which are quite unmistakable in style, with a strange *nostalgie de nuit.*

189. HENRY MOORE (*b.* 1898). The Family. 1945. Bronze. 7 in. high. *London, Tate Gallery.*

190. ENGLISH SCHOOL, MID-EIGHTEENTH CENTURY. Conversation piece: a lady winding wool and a gentleman drawing. *c.* 1745. Oil on canvas. 45¼ × 38¼ in. *Upton House, Banbury: The Viscount Bearsted.*

This painting has been attributed to Arthur Pond (1705–58), but in the opinion of Professor Ellis Waterhouse and Mr. Ralph Edwards is more likely to be the work of Pieter van Bleeck.

195. RAMSAY RICHARD REINAGLE, R.A. (1775–1862). A gentleman in a landscape, with white horse and dogs. 1816. Oil on canvas. 30 × 25 in. *London, Messrs. M. Bernard.*

196. CAPITAL OF A DECORATED COLUMN in the Chapter House, Southwell, Nottinghamshire. *c.* 1300. Photograph by Edwin Smith.

201. ALBRECHT DÜRER (1471–1528). Hands in adoration. 1508. Brush drawing with white lights, on blue ground. 11½ × 7¾ in. *Vienna, Albertina Collection.*

This is a study for the Heller altar-piece. A portion of the dark background at the top of the sheet has been omitted here in order to give a larger reproduction.

202. JOHN ZOFFANY, R.A. (1733–1810). Mrs. Oswald. *c.* 1770. Oil on canvas. 89¼ × 62½ in. *London, National Gallery.*

211. ROGIER VAN DER WEYDEN (*c.* 1400–64). The Magdalen. Oil on panel. 24 × 20½ in. *London, National Gallery.*

Until last year, almost all the background was heavily over-painted. This is the first colour reproduction to reveal the original detail behind the figure of the Magdalen. The cleaning has also revealed that the work is a part of a larger picture.

212. BEN NICHOLSON (*b.* 1894). Abstract painting. May 1957, Aegina. Oil on board. 22 × 19½ in. *London, Gimpels Fils.*

217. DIRK BOUTS (1400–75). Portrait of a man. 1462. Oil on panel. 12½ × 8 in. *London, National Gallery.*

Dirk Bouts, born at Haarlem, was a follower of the Van Eycks and worked for a time under Rogier van der Weyden. This painting used to be attributed to Memling.

218. PHOTOGRAPH BY CLARENCE PONTING. Frost on a window pane.

223. EDGAR DEGAS (1834–1917). An old peasant woman. 1857. Oil on canvas. 40×30 in. *Sir Chester Beatty, Collection of Edith Beatty.* (Copyright S.P.A.D.E.M. Paris.)

224. STAFFORDSHIRE POTTERY GROUP. A man and his wife. *c.* 1840. 6½ in. high. *London, Victoria and Albert Museum.*

233. DOMENICO THEOTOCOPOULOS, known as EL GRECO (1541–1614). The Burial of Count Orgaz (Detail). 1586. Oil on canvas. 192×142 in. *Toledo, Church of Santo Tomé.*

The vast composition from which this detail is reproduced was described by El Greco himself as 'my sublime work'. It commemorates the burial, in the fourteenth century, of the pious Count of Orgaz, Don Gonzales Ruiz, when St. Stephen and St. Augustine miraculously descended from heaven and placed the dead knight in his sepulchre. The detail reproduced is from the upper part of the picture, high above the two saints and the assembled nobles and clerics, and shows the infant soul of the dead grandee, carried by an angel, ascending towards Christ, with the Virgin on the left and John the Baptist on the right.

234. MONUMENT TO SIR WILLIAM DYER. 1641. Alabaster and black marble. *Church of St. Denys, Colmworth, Bedfordshire.*

Sir William Dyer died in 1621 at the age of thirty-six, but this fine monument was not erected by his widow until 1641. The verses by her, from which a passage is quoted on page 235, are carved in black marble behind the reclining effigies. The seven Dyer children are seen in effigy at the front of the tomb.

239. TERRACOTTA RELIEF. Madonna and child. Florentine, early sixteenth century. 27×21 in. *Leeds, Temple Newsam House.*

240. ABRAHAM PETHER (1756–1812). The Snowdrop. Mezzotint by Ward from Robert Thornton's *Temple of Flora*, 1799–1807. 19¼×13¾ in. *London, Messrs. Heywood Hill Ltd.*

Endpapers. PLASTERWORK. Adam and Eve. Detail from seventeenth-century plaster ceiling in the Long Gallery at Lanhydrock, Cornwall. Photograph by the National Buildings Record. *National Trust.*

INDEX TO AUTHORS AND ARTISTS